W9-AVK-516

100 GREATEST TV STARS OF OUR TIME

CONTENTS

STAFF
Editor Elizabeth Sporkin *Senior Editor* Richard Burgheim *Writers* Michael A. Lipton, Elizabeth O'Brien Moore, Joanna Powell, J.D. Reed, Lisa Russell, Ericka Sóuter, Michelle Tan, Jennifer Wulff *Chief of Reporters* Randy Vest *Researchers* Laura Downey, Rennie Dyball, Toby Kahn, Ericka Sóuter *Picture Editor* Brian Belovitch *Art Director* Gregory Monfries *Designers* Jean Beinart, Ronnie Brandwein-Keats *Scanner* Rashida Morgan *Imaging Specialist* Omar Martinez *Copy Editor* Lance Kaplan *Editorial Operations* Peter Herbert (Director), Helen Russell (Manager), George W. Hill, John A. Silva, Mauricio Vale, Peter Zambouros
Special thanks to: Jane Bealer, Will Becker, Victoria Boughton, Robert Britton, Jennifer Broughel, Jessica Bryan, Luciana Chang, Sal Covarrubias, Orpha Davis, Urbano DelValle, Maura Foley, Margery Frohlinger, Patricia Hustoo, John Luisi, Maddy Miller, Charles Nelson, Lillian Nici, Susan Radlauer, Deborah Ratel, Mikema Reape, Patricia Rommeney, Annette Rusin, Jack Styczynski, Gail Toivanen, Céline Wojtala, Patrick Yang

TIME INC. HOME ENTERTAINMENT
President Rob Gursha *Vice President, Branded Businesses* David Arfine *Vice President, New Product Development* Richard Fraiman *Executive Director, Marketing Services* Carol Pittard *Director, Retail & Special Sales* Tom Mifsud *Director of Finance* Tricia Griffin *Brand Manager* Niki Whelan *Prepress Manager* Emily Rabin *Associate Book Production Manager* Suzanne Janso *Associate Product Manager* Linda Frisbie *Special thanks to:* Bozena Bannett, Robert Dente, Gina Di Meglio, Anne-Michelle Gallero, Peter Harper, Robert Marasco, Natalie McCrea, Jonathan Polsky, Mary Jane Rigoroso, Steven Sandonato

SARAH JESSICA PARKER

 ISBN: 1-931933-87-1. Library of Congress Control Number: 2003100213. People Books is a trademark of Time Inc. We welcome your comments and suggestions about People Books. Please write to us at People Books, Attention: Book Editors, P.O. Box 11016, Des Moines, IA 50336-1016. If you would like to order any of our hardcover Collector's Edition books, please call us at 1-800-327-6388 (Monday through Friday, 7:00 a.m.–8:00 p.m., or Saturday, 7:00 a.m.– 6:00 p.m. Central Time).

100 GREATEST TV STARS 100 GREATEST TV STARS 100 GREATEST TV ST

GREATEST TV STARS 100 GREATEST TV STARS 100 GREATEST TV STARS

TV stardom can be fickle and fleeting. Or it can last, seemingly, forever. Who knew, back in 1974, PEOPLE's first year, that such cover subjects as Johnny Carson, Carol Burnett and Barbara Walters would endure over the next three decades—or that Jennifer Aniston, then a kid probably watching *Romper Room,* would adorn the front of this book? In selecting the 100 small-screen icons that helped define the PEOPLE era, the editors considered not just the ratings toppers but also the trendsetters who helped transform our times: career women (Mary Tyler Moore), superdads (Bill Cosby), single moms (Candice Bergen) and social commentators (Oprah Winfrey). Even their faces wielded influence: Don Johnson's stubble, Luke Perry's sideburns. And catchphrases like "Aaaay!" "D'oh!" and "Nanu-nanu" still reverberate in our ears. So forget (as you likely will) the Bachelorettes and Joe Millionaires of today's reality-drenched TV. Here are the real Survivors, the bona fide American Idols of our memories and dreams.

WHETHER THEY WERE *ALL IN THE FAMILY* OR BECAME OUR WEEKLY BEST *FRIENDS,* THESE LARGER-THAN-LIFE MAESTROS OF THE MEDIUM HELPED PUT THE MUST-SEE IN TV

THE ICONS

JENNIFER ANISTON

Born: February 11, 1969

THE PEOPLE'S CRUSH The haircut was the first thing we noticed. But after nine seasons of Friendship, Jennifer Aniston proved to be much more than "the Rachel." Hailed as nothing less than the Mary Tyler Moore of her generation, the California-born, Manhattan-bred Aniston has made her character, Rachel Green, the Friend the rest of the cast orbits around, firmly establishing the NBC show in the Nielsen Top 10. Since the pilot, when she first burst into Central Perk on the lam from her own wedding, millions of fans were hooked as Rachel forged a career (from Central Perk's worst waitress to a star fashion buyer), fell in and out of love and redefined motherhood as prime time's hottest single mom. "It's not just Rachel's situation people connect to," Aniston said during her character's coffee-slinging days. "It's her essence." Like MTM before her, the actress imbued her babe-in-the-big-city with an endearing insecurity and a coltish charm to take over as TV's sitcom queen and collect an Emmy and a $1 million-per-episode paycheck. "What makes her extraordinary is that she can do emotional stuff in a funny way, and funny stuff in a way that feels so moving," said executive producer David Crane. Aniston, who shares a $13.5 million Beverly Hills manse with heartthrob hubby Brad Pitt, is also doing the emotional and funny stuff in films like 2002's *The Good Girl* and this year's *Bruce Almighty.* And when *Friends* ends? "I'd like to travel. I'd like to have a family. I'd like to do it all," she said recently. Pitt is convinced. "I've always known she was amazing," he said. "It just seems like the rest of the world is waking up to what has been there all along."

BILL COSBY

Born: July 12, 1937

THE FATHER FIGURE When *The Cosby Show* first hit the air in 1984, critics complained that the NBC sitcom, which featured Bill Cosby as a doctor raising five children with his lawyer wife (Phylicia Rashad), was unrealistic. "People would say, 'That's not a real black family,' " recalled Tempestt Bledsoe, who played daughter Vanessa. In fact, the Huxtables were originally scripted as blue-collar, but Cosby sought to fight stereotypes, not feed them. "I wanted a show that presented black people in a light you don't often see," he said. Black or white, rich or poor, what made viewers tune in for eight years was that the Huxtables were, above all else, a family headed by Cosby. With his deadpan delivery, warmth, wisdom and natural rapport with anyone under voting age, he became a father to a population much vaster than his TV kids. For four years, in fact, the series topped the Nielsens before a decline hastened by the slotting opposite it of another family showcase: *The Simpsons.*

Raised with three brothers in the Philadelphia projects by his mom, a maid (his father left home when he was 9), Cosby did not enjoy a Huxtable-like youth. He failed 10th grade twice and joined the Navy, but eventually won a football scholarship to Temple University and earned a Ph.D. in education. In 1965 he was the first African-American cast as a lead in a prime-time drama series, *I Spy,* opposite Robert Culp, for which he won three of his four Emmys. (He has also earned 9 Grammys and 16 People's Choice awards.) Whether lending his voice to *Fat Albert and the Cosby Kids* or an ear to *Kids Say the Darndest Things,* Cosby built a franchise—and a net worth estimated at $400 million. Tragedy struck during the run of his last sitcom, CBS's *Cosby.* His son Ennis (he also has four daughters with his wife of 39 years, Camille) was murdered during an attempted robbery by the side of a highway in 1997. That same day, a woman claiming to be his daughter tried to extort $40 million from him. Cosby soon admitted to once having an affair with the girl's mother, but paternity remains unproven. The news didn't dim his popularity, and his comedy tours continue to sell out. "People always say, 'Why are you still working?' " he noted recently. "My answer is that it isn't about money. It's about accepting the challenges of one's own ideas and pursuing the excitement of discovery." Or put more succinctly: "I simply love to perform."

FUNNY FACE With a trademark tug of her ear or a side-splitting Tarzan yell, the rubber-faced comedian dispensed homey hilarity on *The Carol Burnett Show* (1967-78), collecting three Emmys at a time when variety shows were dying. "I wasn't afraid to look awful," she explained of her success. "Sometimes we'd have a sketch that wasn't good, but you put a wig on, boobs hanging down to your navel, and suddenly . . ." Also she had a genius for mimicry and showbiz spoofs ("Mildred Fierce," "As the Stomach Turns") plus a gifted "family" of regulars including Harvey Korman and Vicki Lawrence. Behind the humor was a touching humanity stemming from Burnett's tough, impoverished childhood in L.A. The daughter of alcoholics, she escaped and found her comic calling at UCLA. Eventually, Burnett married her producer, Joe Hamilton (they divorced after two decades), and had three daughters. One of her bleakest moments came in January 2002 when her oldest, Carrie, died of lung cancer at age 38. "Carol has been through more trauma in her life than anybody deserves," said friend Lucie Arnaz. A brighter coda is Burnett's third marriage, to music contractor Brian Miller, whom she wed in 2001, just days before her TV reunion special drew an astonishing 30 million viewers. As Charles Grodin, her costar in the '80s miniseries *Fresno,* declared: "If there is someone more popular in this country than Carol Burnett, I would like to know who that is."

CAROL BURNETT

Born: April 26, 1933

FARRAH FAWCETT

Born: February 2, 1947

THE PINUP For a nation still recovering from Vietnam and Watergate, *Charlie's Angels* was the antidote. It was sexy, diverting and sometimes silly, but its trio of comely, scantily clad female private eyes included one who came to epitomize the times: Farrah Fawcett, a feather-haired blonde with a gleaming smile as wide as her native Texas. By the end of her first and only full season (1976-77) on the hit series, the shampoo model—then married to actor Lee Majors, TV's Six Million Dollar Man—had become a full-fledged phenomenon, a marketing dream machine of lunchboxes and dolls, not to mention an iconic swimsuit poster that hung on some 8 million walls. "I think it's better to have that kind of furor around you when it's about your work, but I don't know if it will ever be like that for me," admitted Fawcett, whose former manager summed up her popularity in one word: "nipples." Seven years of lackluster film work followed before Fawcett (split from Majors in 1982) finally earned critical recognition with a TV movie, *The Burning Bed,* playing a battered wife who takes revenge on an abusive husband. Many saw parallels to her own stormy 17-year relationship with actor Ryan O'Neal (with whom she has a son). It ended in '97, but recently they resumed playing tennis together. In the late 1990s a disastrous appearance on David Letterman's *Late Show,* in which she seemed incoherent, and a *Playboy* video in which the former college art major—then 50—rolled her nude, paint-covered body on canvas hinted at the darker side of the reclusive woman once called a "radiant exemplar of American sunshine." If so, she kept it mostly to herself. "After all her years of being famous, very few people know much about her," said her agent, Todd Harris. "It's almost as if no one can ever get past that hair and that smile."

Born: December 17, 1989

HOMER SIMPSON

DADDY D'OH In just one generation and a giant leap of the imagination, the TV art advanced from Fred Flintstone to Homer Simpson, from *Father Knows Best* to Father Knows Nada. The true paterfamilias of *The Simpsons* was, of course, Matt Groening, 49, corrosive cartoonist of the underground strip *Life in Hell*. Groening named Homer and Marge after his own parents, and he has a son Homer (but not a Bart, which is an anagram of "brat"). After a test spot on *The Tracey Ullman Show, The Simpsons* landed its own FOX slot in 1989. Groening, said programming VP Mike Darnell, "took these yellow-skinned, big-eyed, weird-looking characters and made them feel more like a real family than ones in most live-action sitcoms." It wasn't long before Dustin Hoffman, Elizabeth Taylor and even Johnny Carson were vying to create guest voices (Dan Castellaneta does Homer), and Homer's bleat "d'oh" is enshrined in *The Oxford English Dictionary.* As one critic wrote: "*The Simpsons* is to today's prime time what Manet's *Olympia* was to modern art." That might be lost on Homer, but he would be proud. He never smartened up, just as daughter Lisa, keen as she is, will likely still be in second grade in 2005, when *The Simpsons* becomes the longest-running comedy in TV history, replacing, yes, *Ozzie and Harriet*.

JOHNNY CARSON

Born: October 23, 1925

THE NATURAL "Johnny Carson has done more to ruin America's love life than anyone else in the country," Dr. Ruth once said. For whatever reason, the baby boom was winding down when he replaced Jack Paar and began his 30-year reign on *The Tonight Show.* Whether tending to an incontinent marmoset or an overexcited Robin Williams or yukking it up in a Tarzan sketch, the Nebraska-raised Carson became America's perfect nightcap, a perky, stainless-steel pixie with eyes that twinkled like Christmas lights. Though quick with a quip or a naughty double entendre, he was also a great listener. "You could throw shots at him and he always came back making you look good," said frequent visitor Don Rickles. As sidekick Ed McMahon added, "Johnny Carson was far more comfortable in front of millions of people than he ever was with a small group." Another source once described his private life as "the best-kept secret since the Coca-Cola formula." Since retiring, he has stayed close to home in Malibu, rarely venturing out except for trips on his 130-ft. yacht with fourth wife Alexis, whom he wed in 1987. Returning to television has apparently never tempted him. "I don't know anyone other than Cary Grant who left the stage with such dignity and grace," said TV honcho Barry Diller. After taking his final phantom golf swing in 1992, Carson was succeeded, of course, by Jay Leno, but he will never be replaced as the unconquerable King of Late Night. "The only good thing about being clobbered by Johnny Carson is that you are forever mentioned in the same breath," said Alan Thicke, whose *Thicke of the Night* lasted nine months opposite Carson. "He is simply the best there was. He'll have his own wing in the Talk Show Hall of Fame—a monument to wit, charm, relatability and sophistication."

CARROLL O'CONNOR

Born: August 2, 1924 Died: June 21, 2001

ARMCHAIR ARCHETYPE "Archie Bunker wasn't very likable," conceded Carroll O'Connor, who played the cantankerous crank for 12 years. "But everyone loved him." Everyone also loved O'Connor. "Carroll O'Connor as Archie Bunker," said *All in the Family* creator Norman Lear, "was a genius at work." When the show premiered in 1971, tackling prime-time taboos like bigotry, rape and homosexuality, the veteran Bronx-born actor believed it a "noble" but doomed experiment. More than 50 million weekly viewers proved him wrong as he wrangled with dingbat wife Edith (Jean Stapleton), liberal daughter Gloria (Sally Struthers) and meathead son-in-law Mike (Rob Reiner). The series spun off three major sitcoms and earned O'Connor four Emmys; he took home a fifth as a southern police chief in *In the Heat of the Night.* In 1995 life took a tragic turn when Hugh O'Connor, his son with his wife of nearly 50 years, Nancy, killed himself after a long battle with drug addiction, and O'Connor became a national voice against substance abuse. "He was one of the most intelligent and generous people I have ever worked with," said Stapleton. "When I have the occasion to catch a rerun, I am reminded of his marvelous talent and humor." Those were the days.

INTERVIEWER EXTRAORDINAIRE It wasn't easy for Barbara Walters to get on air herself, much less persuade so many A-list stars to join her. She became TV's most famous interviewer through that oldest of journalistic requisites: doggedness. "I'm an awful nag," she once said. The Boston-born daughter of a nightclub impresario, Walters paid dues for 13 years as a writer and reporter on NBC's *Today* but wasn't deemed appealing enough to cohost until 1974. She wasn't considered experienced enough to become a network news anchor either, but she got that job too—becoming in 1976 the first female in the job for a then record $1 million. Her ABC co-anchor Harry Reasoner was unwelcoming, and one critic sniped, "Is Barbara a journalist or is she Cher?" She also became a favorite parody subject of Gilda Radner, but that was perhaps a compliment. If her questions were drippingly sincere ("When was the last time you cried?"), the celebs Walters lured to her couch—from Fidel Castro to Monica Lewinsky—have been eerily forthcoming. She has ridden a motorcycle with Stallone, played drums with Ringo and pondered Clint Eastwood's "tight rear end." Still snagging the big "gets" for her Oscar specials, *20/20* and her brainchild *The View,* the twice-divorced mother of one has "had a tough life . . . and can empathize," P.R. maven Howard Rubenstein observed. "There's no one better."

BARBARA WALTERS

Born: September 25, 1931

OPRAH WINFREY

Born: January 29, 1954

AMERICA'S GIRLFRIEND The folks at her church in rural Mississippi took notice when 3-year-old Oprah Winfrey recited Bible stories to the congregation. "This child sure can talk," they'd tell her grandmother Hattie Mae. Little did they know. Since 1985, when *AM Chicago* was renamed *The Oprah Winfrey Show,* Hattie Mae's grandchild has parlayed her girlhood gift of gab into the most popular talk show in TV history, racking up 35 Emmys and becoming one of the most powerful—and richest—women on the planet. Fans are fascinated by the trappings—private chef, Gulfstream jet, luxurious homes. But true Oprah addicts love her more for what she overcame. Born illegitimate and poor, she survived sexual abuse, rape and the death of an infant she bore at age 14. "It's a wonder she's not off in a corner drooling," longtime friend Gayle King has said. Instead, after a teenage stay with her disciplinarian dad in Nashville, she got an early shot as an anchor in Baltimore. Then, in Chicago, she found her niche as the nation's everywoman, openly sharing her fears and foibles (even pulling a wagon load of animal fat onstage to represent the 67 pounds she shed in 1988). "Oprah is still struggling with the same things as her viewers," noted a former producer. "She's not perfect, but she wants to be." As speculation swirls over whether she will ultimately wed her "permanent fiancé," P.R. exec Stedman Graham, the billionaire tycoon casts an ever-widening net: donating millions to charity, producing TV movies (such as *Tuesdays with Morrie*), launching TV spin-offs like *Dr. Phil,* cofounding the Oxygen cable network and editing her successful O magazine. "If I can't take a risk, nobody can," Winfrey has said. "With fame, notoriety, credibility, if you can't have the courage to stand up and speak out for what you truly believe in, then it means nothing."

FAVORITE SON It was 1982, the dawning of the Me Decade, and Michael J. Fox's evocation of an unabashed yuppie made greed and self-absorption seem, well, "something awesome," said Gary David Goldberg, creator of NBC's *Family Ties*. "The moments when Michael was out there were like a white light." His costars were similarly dazzled. "He was flawless," said *Ties* mom Meredith Baxter. Stealing a show when he was originally intended to be a mere second banana, Fox turned it into a Top 10 perennial, and suddenly a 5'4" regular guy from Canada was Hollywood's hottest—and most humble—import. "I got sick of turning on the TV and seeing my face," he said. Three Emmys and one movie smash later (1985's *Back to the Future*), Fox and company cut *Ties* in 1989, and he focused on films before returning to TV in 1996 on ABC's *Spin City*. Once again Fox took a slightly unsavory character—a New York City deputy mayor he called "borderline reprehensible"—and made him human. "Our research said Michael J. Fox could be the Son of Sam and he could pull it off," said then-ABC exec Ted Harbert. "He exudes likability." He won a fourth Emmy before leaving the show in 2000 to help find a cure for Parkinson's disease, which he has battled since 1991. With homes in New York City and rural Connecticut, the actor who titled his 2002 memoir *Lucky Man* now spends his time with his family—actress wife Tracy Pollan and their four children—and the Michael J. Fox Foundation for Parkinson's Research.

MICHAEL J. FOX

Born: June 9, 1961

JERRY SEINFELD

Born: April 29, 1954

MASTER OF HIS DOMAIN Dubbed the show about nothing, his anti-sitcom became a seismic something. Centered around the lives of four neurotic, self-centered New Yorkers, *Seinfeld* was, for nine brilliant seasons, a part of America's national conversation. Its catchphrases like "yada yada yada" and "sponge-worthy" joined the vernacular. "No hugs, no learning" was co-creator Larry David's credo for the show. It dealt with issues like waiting for a table at a restaurant, losing a car in a parking lot or ordering a bowl of soup, but such mundane occurrences became memorable, thanks to the offbeat, keenly observant comedy style of headliner Seinfeld. "Some people look at the newspaper and see stories," he once said. "I see the paper and the ink and the way it's folded."

A native of Long Island and grad of New York's Queens College, Seinfeld struggled into the stand-up circuit, supporting himself selling lightbulbs over the phone and costume jewelry from a collapsible cart. In 1989, eight years after his first of 30-odd appearances on *Tonight,* he finally got his own show. NBC ended up earning $200 million a year from the high-rated sitcom, even while paying Seinfeld $1 million an episode by the final season. Living on New York's Upper West Side in a megamillion duplex apartment, Seinfeld, whose last episode was watched by 76 million, is now playing to a smaller crowd: wife of 3½ years Jessica, their daughter Sascha and son Julian Kal. Though he made a brief return to stand-up in 2001, touring the country and documenting it in the 2002 film *Comedian,* Seinfeld has no immediate plans to reappear on the small or the big screen. "I'll tell you something," he once said. "I'd rather say something that people would quote as a great line that I thought of than win an Oscar." Not that there's anything wrong with that.

Born: October 31, 1936 Died: July 1, 1991

MICHAEL LANDON

PROUD PAPA Michael Landon had an unparalleled, three-decade run atop the TV heap, but he is best remembered for the second of his three back-to-back smash series: the determinedly heartwarming *Little House on the Prairie.* In the eight years he played resolute papa Charles Ingalls (after 14 years as *Bonanza*'s "Little Joe" Cartwright), the actor also emerged as a writer and producer, with a clear vision of his message for America. "I believe in God . . . family . . . truth between people . . . [and] the power of love," Landon said unapologetically. ("Before we started a scene he would always ask, 'Have you finished your homework?' " recalled teen cast member David Friedman.) The same homespun virtues infused his next series, *Highway to Heaven.* Though critics scoffed at the show ("They were more interested in reviewing my hair," he said), Landon's high ratings and low cost overruns made true believers of the TV brass. "My dream network," said NBC's late president Brandon Tartikoff, "would be 22 hours of talents like his." Born Eugene Maurice Orowitz, he had suffered through a miserable childhood in New Jersey but had finally found a long-sought, harmonious home life by the time he was diagnosed with pancreatic cancer in 1991. Three months later, after a graceful fight ("I never did the standing-on-a-hilltop-and-screaming kind of thing"), Landon died, at 54, with his third wife, Cindy, by his side and all nine of his children downstairs in his Malibu home. "It's not like I've missed a hell of a lot," he declared. "I've had a pretty good lick here."

MARY TYLER MOORE

Born: December 29, 1936

HAIL MARY Men wanted to marry her. Women wanted to *be* her. But America's Sweetheart is a one-woman job, and Mary Tyler Moore had the best credentials. "She was the girl everyone fell in love with," said James L. Brooks, co-creator of the CBS series. "Then she became this icon of a new age, this independent woman." With that famous toss of her hat, spunky Mary Richards embodied the "liberated" single career woman of the '70s, paving the way for the likes of Murphy Brown and Ally McBeal. "She was a woman who stood up for herself whenever she spotted any inequity, but who wasn't going to push it to the edge," said the Brooklyn-born Moore. "She made little squeaks and noises and was among the first to do so." A two-time Emmy winner as Laura Petrie, the doting (if sometimes dotty) wife she played for five years on *The Dick Van Dyke Show,* Moore was prepared to headline a zany cast (Ed Asner, Valerie Harper, Gavin MacLeod, Cloris Leachman and Ted Knight) whose antics kept viewers tuned to what is often called TV's most beloved sitcom. In its seven years the show amassed 29 Emmys (four for Moore) and spun off *Rhoda, Phyllis* and *Lou Grant.* When the series ended in 1977, Moore deliberately left Mary Richards behind, earning an Oscar nod for her role as the bloodless Wasp mom in 1980's *Ordinary People.* Her personal life took some very un-Mary-like turns as well, with a divorce (from Grant Tinker, with whom she'd founded the MTM production company), rehab at the Betty Ford Center and the loss of her only son, Richie, to a self-inflicted gunshot wound at 24. Sharing homes in Manhattan and Upstate New York with her third husband, cardiologist Robert Levine, she stays busy with stage, film and TV roles—none of which, however, are likely to inspire a tribute like the 6-ft. bronze statue of her hat-tossing alter ego now adorning a Minneapolis mall. "A lot of people have said, 'Gosh, when I used to watch you, I wanted to be like you—like Mary Richards,'" said Moore. "And my answer has always been, 'So did I.'"

JOHN BELUSHI

Born: January 24, 1949 Died: March 5, 1982

A TRAGIC COMIC As the main maniac on NBC's *Saturday Night Live* from 1975 to 1979, John Belushi made America laugh doing things never seen before on TV. He jammed cigars up his nose, smashed beer cans against his forehead, took flying somersaults and landed smack on his coccyx. He immortalized the samurai sandwich man and outlaw Killer Bee ("Your pollen or your wife, Señor!"), invented the diner where patrons could get only a "cheezbugga, cheezbugga" and delivered a lung-shredding impersonation of Joe Cocker. But as the most outrageous member of SNL's wild-and-crazy original cast, Belushi came to yearn for higher challenge. "What we are, man, is actors . . . not dressing like f------ bees!" he complained. He proved his point on the big screen. As grunting, belching frat boy Bluto Blutarsky in the 1978 smash *Animal House,* he bloomed into what one critic called "the funniest fat comic actor since Jackie Gleason." The son of an Albanian immigrant who owned a string of eateries, he grew up in a Chicago suburb with three siblings (including actor brother James). A popular athlete, he married his high school sweetheart, Judy Jacklin, and at 22 Belushi became the youngest performer ever hired by the Second City improv troupe. There he became pals with future *SNL* troupers Gilda Radner and Dan Aykroyd, with whom he would partner for the Blues Brothers soul-singing act and movie. Right from the start, Belushi was a child of chaos, a poet of explosions. If a scene lagged, he might leap to the footlights and scream, "Eat a bowl of s---!" If table talk proved less than exhilarating, he might suddenly sneeze into a companion's soup. And if he saw a woman in tight jeans, he'd dart up behind her and bite her butt. In hindsight, it's arguable that Belushi was on a death trip. He ate like a python, engulfing three or four meals at a single sitting. And his appetite for drugs, especially cocaine, grew lethal as he struggled to cope with success. It all ended, at age 33, in bungalow 3 of L.A.'s Chateau Marmont hotel, when he died of an overdose after drug supplier Cathy Smith injected him with a coke-and-heroin "speedball." In *Wired,* his biographer, Bob Woodward, wrote Belushi's epitaph: "He made us laugh, and now he can make us think." An admirer's hand-lettered sign beside his grave on the island of Martha's Vineyard conveyed a similar sentiment: "HE COULD HAVE GIVEN US A LOT MORE LAUGHS . . . BUT NOOOOOOO."

MAKING THEIR MARK

McBEAL, MacGYVER, ELLEN . . . PLAYING MORE THAN JUST PARTS, THEY CREATED ROLE MODELS THAT DEFINED OUR TIMES OR CHANGED OUR LOOK, OR OUTLOOK. AND *AAAAY*—SOMETIMES THEY EVEN WOUND UP PART OF THE LINGO

HENRY WINKLER

Born: October 30, 1945

MALT-SHOP MACHO The Fonz was not supposed to be the center of attention—that was the mission of Richie Cunningham (Ron Howard). But as soon as Henry Winkler let out his first "Aaaay," *Happy Days* viewers became as smitten with him as were the poodle-skirted honeys at Arnold's malt shop. "I went from getting one letter from my mom to 50,000 fan letters," Winkler recalled. "I understood from that point on that I wouldn't have to eat the blue-plate special anymore." The 5'7" Yale drama school grad was an unlikely choice for the role of a greaser dropout on the '50s-set sitcom. "His brand of coolness wasn't about toughness," said Howard, a child TV star who wound up a major film director. "It was about being totally collected and on top of every situation." During the show's 10-year run, Winkler's image appeared on socks, underwear, combs, perfume, bubblegum and kids' lunchboxes from here to Japan. After *Happy Days,* the actor from New York City produced *MacGyver* and tried his hand at directing. More recently, he has taken guest gigs on shows like *The Practice* (for which he was nominated for an Emmy) and has appeared on Broadway and in films like *The Waterboy.* Living in Los Angeles with wife Stacey, with whom he has two children, Zoe and Max, Winkler is still best known for that first breakthrough role, but if you happen to greet him as Fonzie on the street, he won't tell you to sit on it. "To have people like my work, even if it's my old work," he said recently, "I can ask for nothing nicer than that."

ALAN ALDA

Born: January 28, 1936

MR. SENSITIVE "We'll mix heavy stuff with light stuff," vowed Alan Alda. "The brutality of war combined with the desire to heal—no other comedy on TV has such a powerful basis." So mighty was it that in 1983, 11 seasons later, *M*A*S*H*'s finale drew a then-record 125 million U.S. viewers. As Korean War surgeon Benjamin Franklin "Hawkeye" Pierce, the Manhattan-born Alda was the maestro of that success, melding decency with wit and rebelliousness, setting the tone for the most original program of its time. Costar Loretta Swit (Hotlips Houlihan) called him "the most multitalented and versatile person I've ever known." Ironically, Alda, who went on to win five Emmys for acting, writing and directing the series, considered passing on the TV adaptation of the movie classic except for the opportunity "to make my position clear against war." Offscreen he stumped for many other causes, women's rights in particular, becoming a poster boy for the sensitive male. Rather than relocate to L.A., he stayed in New Jersey with Arlene, his photographer wife of 46 years, and their three daughters. He has continued to act, write and direct (*The Four Seasons* and *Betsy's Wedding*) and even tried to break the nice-guy mold by playing against type (in HBO's *And the Band Played On* and Woody Allen's *Crimes and Misdemeanors*). It didn't totally work. "It's too bad I'm not as wonderful a person as people say I am," Alda noted, "because the world could use a few good people like that."

CANDICE BERGEN

Born: May 9, 1946

BAD, BAD MURPHY BROWN She never wanted to be just another pretty face, and in the smart, acerbic title role of the CBS sitcom *Murphy Brown,* Candice Bergen found her own prime time—winning five Emmys and sparking a national debate. When Murphy chose to give birth out of wedlock in 1992, Vice President Dan Quayle charged that the character mocked "the importance of fathers by bearing a child alone and calling it just another lifestyle choice." To millions of viewers, Bergen often blurred with the beautiful, barb-slinging reporter she played, a Mike-Wallace-in-a-dress. But offscreen the actress proved more traditional, saying, "Work was never my first priority." After growing up in Beverly Hills, the daughter of famed ventriloquist Edgar Bergen and model Frances Westerman, she fell into acting in the late '60s and the '70s—her flawless looks locking her into ice-queen movie roles such as *Carnal Knowledge* and *Oliver's Story.* At the same time, she made her mark as a photojournalist and articulate feminist-activist. In 1980 she wed eminent French film director Louis Malle, and when their daughter Chloe was born five years later, she quit acting and devoted herself to full-time motherhood for three years. "I was a mom so late in life," she said, "my daughter was the greatest thing since sliced bread." The family divided their time between Los Angeles and Malle's estate in France in what Bergen called "a halcyon age" until the director died of lymphoma in 1995. After her series ended its 10-season run in 1998, Bergen observed, "I will never be more comfortable than I was with Murphy." She took a two-year hiatus before returning to TV as host of the Oxygen cable channel's prime-time talk show *Exhale.* In 2000 she married New York real estate magnate Marshall Rose and returned to films with *Miss Congeniality* and *Sweet Home Alabama.* She was back in Hollywood, still a strikingly pretty face. But, determinedly, not just another one.

ELLEN DeGENERES

Born: January 26, 1958

GAY GROUNDBREAKER "Good for you. You're gay." And with those historic words (spoken by Oprah Winfrey, playing her therapist), Ellen DeGeneres came out of the closet on a 1997 episode of her sitcom *Ellen*. The droll, self-effacing stand-up comic immediately found herself in a firestorm of controversy over her status as TV's first prime-time lesbian lead and as the very public girlfriend of actress Anne Heche. As the couple's profile soared, *Ellen*'s ratings plummeted—and not only because its newly homocentric plot lines scared away conservatives. "Even gay viewers are saying we're too much in-your-face," admitted exec producer Tim Doyle. In 1998, not long after Elton John, himself openly gay, declared, "We know you're a lesbian. Shut up! Just be funny!" the series ended its four-year run. "I got caught up in it. I got political," DeGeneres admitted. Split from Heche in 2000, she later launched another sitcom that lasted just one season, but by then, thanks to *Ellen,* the small screen was awash in gay roles. "I do think that people respect what I did," noted DeGeneres, slated to begin an NBC talk program this fall. "Even if the show failed, I think there are a lot of people who have changed their minds a little bit."

HOMEMADE HERO He was the unlikeliest of prime-time crime fighters. In fact, the hero of ABC's *MacGyver,* tagged by critics as "an adventure series for thinkers," didn't carry a gun. Instead, Richard Dean Anderson's square-jawed supersleuth vanquished evildoers using "MacGyverisms"—ingenious devices invariably crafted from paper clips and/or chewing gum wrappers. "He's not one of those supermacho guys with their shirts unbuttoned to their navels, who bounce bullets off their chests and wear 400 tons of gold," observed the native Minnesotan. "Our show teaches a different attitude." *MacGyver* became a cultural touchstone from 1985 to 1992, inspiring creative-problem-solving programs in schools and even adding to the lexicon, as both a noun ("He's a regular MacGyver") and a verb ("He MacGyvered it"). Beyond the scriptwriting, there was Anderson's shy sexiness and "aw, shucks" charm, honed on ABC's *General Hospital.* "We went through about 100 actors, and then Richard came in to audition," said *MacGyver* exec producer Henry Winkler. Now sharing his life with longtime girlfriend Apryl Prose and daughter Wylie, Anderson stars as another unconventional good guy on the Sci Fi Channel's *Stargate SG-1.* But there's no escaping his past. In the pilot episode a character said, "It took us 15 years and three supercomputers to MacGyver a system for the gate on Earth."

RICHARD DEAN ANDERSON

Born: January 23, 1950

TWICE AS NICE Sure, they did have a pet pony growing up, but ***Full House*** stars Mary-Kate (left) and Ashley Olsen were not given free rein to splurge on the millions they earned as America's best-loved twins. At 9, they were still expected to clean their rooms before collecting their $5 weekly allowance from parents Dave and Jarnie (a former dancer with the Los Angeles Ballet). "We do everything other kids do," Mary-Kate said at the time. "We go to school, play with our friends, have sleepovers." The fraternal twins (Ashley is older by three minutes) split the role of cutie-pie Michelle from the age of 9 months until the sitcom ended when they were 9. By 1992 their commercial empire Dualstar was founded, to cash in on a popular video and book series, video games, records and dolls that outsell everyone but Barbie. Now with their own clothing, beauty and home-furnishings line at Wal-Mart, they have amassed an estimated $76 million fortune, which will be released from a trust fund once they turn 18. While another show isn't out of the question, their SAT scores mean more to them these days than Q Ratings. "Right now their priority is getting into the college of their choice and finishing their studies," said manager Robert Thorne. "They insisted that all of this was not going to get in the way of them doing all the things that every other teen does."

THE OLSEN TWINS

Born: June 13, 1986

CALISTA FLOCKHART

Born: November 11, 1964

MINI-SHE Maybe it was the almost criminally short skirt. From the moment Calista Flockhart flitted into the courtroom as a neurotic Boston trial attorney, she became the main defendant in the People v. *Ally McBeal*. Was the series, with its unisex bathroom, dancing baby and ironic special effects, as innovative as admirers claimed? Or, as doubters railed, was Flockhart's lovelorn working woman a needy, neurotic nutcase setting feminism back a generation? "She tries to do the right thing and makes a lot of mistakes," observed Flockhart fondly of her TV alter ego. "We all do." The Rutgers-educated New York theater vet is being modest. "There's never a day when I'm writing when I ask myself, 'Can Calista do this?'" said series creator David E. Kelley. "There's nothing she can't do." Thrust into the role of cultural litmus test, the Audrey Hepburnesque Golden Globe winner brushed off criticism of Ally and bore with dignified reserve media speculation that she was anorexic. "The last thing Calista is is fragile," assured costar Greg Germann. "I think, actually, the way she looks has made her incredibly tough." It also helped make the adoptive mother of son Liam a romance regular in the tabs ("I live vicariously through my rumors," she jested). In 2002, shortly before *Ally* ended its five-season run, Flockhart began dating actor Harrison Ford, 61, and appeared markedly less pensive in public. With a perfect mate, she once said, "I intend to spend a lot of time laughing."

CHER

Born: May 20, 1946

OUTRAGEOUS ORIGINAL With her spidery eyelashes and $5,000 Bob Mackie gowns, Cher was the exotic curiosity that put the sizzle in *The Sonny and Cher Comedy Hour* during the nation's troubled early '70s. "Millions of women watched just to see what I was wearing," she wrote in her autobiography, *The First Time*. But fans also tuned in to chortle at Cher's onscreen bickering with her short, seemingly hapless husband, Sonny Bono, and for her wacky recurring sketch characters (including the eternal Vamp, gum-snapping housewife Laverne and pulchritudinous pizzeria waitress Rosa). "She's unconventional in that she says and does what we all wish we could do," observed TV executive Jeff Sagansky. In 1974 Sonny and Cher broke up their marriage as well as their successful singing act and the CBS show. But her solo TV series fizzled, as did Sonny's, and the duo reunited in 1976 for an out-of-wedlock and short-lived *Sonny and Cher Show*. By then she was pregnant with new husband Gregg Allman's baby (Elijah Blue), and much vitriol had passed publicly between the Bonos. She called him "dictatorial, unfaithful, demanding," and they filed dueling eight-figure lawsuits, which were eventually dropped.

But that was all just the overture for the comic opera of Cherilyn Sarkisian, who grew up in hardscrabble El Centro, California, raised by her struggling mother, Georgia Holt. Cher reinvented herself as a rock princess and began acting in film, impressing reviewers and winning a Best Actress Oscar for *Moonstruck*. Meanwhile the tabloids felled forests to chronicle her romances, tattoos, plastic surgeries and the gay-advocacy campaigns of her daughter Chastity. When Bono, by then a congressman, died in a skiing accident in 1998, his ex delivered a eulogy, later explaining, "I couldn't stay angry with Sonny." In 2002, the now legendary diva re-proved her resilience, launching a massive concert tour that she claimed to be her last. "Someone once said, 'The only thing that will be left after a nuclear holocaust is Cher and cockroaches,'" she told *Interview*. "I think that's funny, because, you know, I am a survivor. If I am anything, that's what I am."

LARRY HAGMAN

Born: September 21, 1931

SATAN IN A STETSON On one fall night in 1980, a global audience of some 350 million tuned in for the answer to what had become a cosmic question in 57 countries: Who shot J.R.? (His sister-in-law Kristin did.) Larry Hagman, of course, survived as the deliciously slimy oil baron J(ohn) R(oss) Ewing and led the nighttime soap *Dallas* through 13 raucous years. "I really can't remember half of the people I've slept with, stabbed in the back or driven to suicide," said Hagman—the genial Texas-raised son of actress Mary Martin—who earlier starred in *I Dream of Jeannie.* The dad of two, wed since 1954 to his Swedish-born wife, Maj, attacked the career-defining role with the gusto he once brought to drink (which led to a 1995 liver transplant). Brio intact, he bounced back to declare in his 2001 memoir, "We made greed, treachery and blackmail seem like good, sexy, All-American fun."

Born: September 25, 1968

WILL SMITH

THE CROWN PRINCE He could easily have gone blooey like MC Hammer. Splurging every penny he'd earned from his three rap albums with pal DJ Jazzy Jeff, the Fresh Prince was on his way to becoming a pauper. But just as the IRS began beating on Will Smith's door, so did NBC executives with a sitcom offer: *The Fresh Prince of Bel-Air.* Though the Philadelphia-born Grammy winner had no acting experience, he was ideal for the role of a wisecracking West Philly teen who moves in with a posh uncle and his family. "Will read from a script and nailed it," said former NBC exec Warren Littlefield of his audition. "I sat there thinking, Whoa! Just bottle this guy!" Eau de Will turned into an addictive potion for six seasons, and it was on the set of *Fresh Prince* that Smith met his princess, Jada Pinkett. At 5'0" the actress was deemed too short to play the 6'2" Smith's love interest on the show, but it was no problem offscreen. Wed since 1997, the couple live outside of L.A. with their son Jaden and daughter Willow. (Smith also has a son, Trey, from his first marriage.) But family and films like *Independence Day* and *Men in Black* have hardly sated his ambitions. "I want to do everything," he has said. "Give me about 10 years, I'm going to run for President. If I can squeeze in an NBA championship before that, I'll do it."

SITCOM SENSATIONS

A GUY (OR A GIRL) WALKS INTO A BAR, A DETECTIVE AGENCY, A COFFEE SHOP . . . AND WHEREVER THEY WERE, THE LIKES OF SAM, DIANE, MADDIE AND PHOEBE COULD ALWAYS MAKE US LAUGH—SOMETIMES UNTIL WE CRIED

DEBRA MESSING

Born: August 15, 1968

CLASSY CLOWN That hair! Those eyes! That perfect pratfall! While comparisons to the queen of TV comedy are inevitable—"I call her Juicy, the Jewish Lucille Ball," said *Will & Grace* director James Burrows—Debra Messing isn't buying it. "That's the greatest compliment," she said. "But I'm not delusional. She's untouchable." Maybe, maybe not. The cast marvels at her agile acrobatics as Grace Adler, the straight best friend of Eric McCormack's gay Will on the NBC sitcom hit. "When she throws herself into physical comedy, she holds nothing back," said McCormack. "She'll take a pie in the face in a second." That's what sets her apart from more, well, image-conscious stars. "Debra takes acting very seriously," said McCormack, "but she doesn't take *herself* seriously." Born in Brooklyn, she studied acting at Brandeis University and New York University. A meaty recurring role on *NYPD Blue* led to a starring gig on FOX's short-lived *Ned and Stacey,* which in 1998 culminated in *Will & Grace*—and two Emmy nominations. Are Oscar nods far off? Woody Allen, who cast her in two films, found Messing "a natural comedian." For now, though, the actress calls her life—on *W&G* and in L.A. with actor-screenwriter hubby Daniel Zelman—"unbelievably miraculous."

KELSEY GRAMMER

Born: February 21, 1955

DR. FEEL GOOD Leaving the cozy confines of a Boston bar, where everybody knew his name, for a Seattle coffee shop, where no one did, Frasier Crane—and Kelsey Grammer—gambled that viewers would follow him. He and NBC bet right. For 10 years the five-time Emmy-winning *Frasier* has been a critical and mainstream hit, making Grammer perhaps the only star in the hugely popular *Cheers* ensemble who shines brighter now than then. "Frasier is enormously human," he said, explaining the appeal of the pompous radio call-in psychiatrist. "People recognize themselves in him, and are charmed by his willingness to fail. He just throws himself into life." The same could be said for Grammer, who turned what was intended to be a six-week stint on *Cheers* into a landmark characterization, which has earned him three Emmys as well as a TV record $1.6 million per episode. As good as the role has been to him, the actor couldn't be more different from the sherry-sipping, opera-loving, designer-suit-wearing prig. "He is the most un-uptight person on earth," said costar Peri Gilpin (Roz Doyle). "He's got a silly sense of humor and comes to work in shorts and flip-flops." Grammer's zest for life had a dark side, though, and he struggled with drug and alcohol abuse for years. "I've always been my own worst enemy," he admitted. "I can undermine myself better than anyone else." His troubles started early. He was raised in New Jersey by his mother and grandparents after his parents divorced when he was just 2. By the time he turned 25, he had endured the murder of his estranged father, the rape and murder of his younger sister and the death of two half brothers in a scuba-diving accident. His love life proved turbulent as well. Divorced twice, he now lives in L.A. with his wife of six years, former *Playboy* model Camille Donatacci, and their toddler Mason Olivia. (He also has two other daughters.) "I went through my problems, but I'm in a different place now," he said. He dabbles in Shakespeare and feature films—and even provides the voice of sociopath Sideshow Bob on *The Simpsons*—but it's clear *Frasier* is his first love. "He's endearing because he's flawed," said Grammer, sounding as if he might be contemplating his own evolving persona. "He's a good man."

Born: July 30, 1956

DELTA BURKE

FEISTY LADY Being cast as Suzanne Sugarbaker, *Designing Women*'s sassy southern beauty queen turned decorator, was not a stretch. Delta Burke was a sassy former Miss Florida herself. The part won her two Emmy nominations—and a rep as a demanding diva after a very public feud with the show's creators. (Burke claimed it was over her weight gain, but executive producer Linda Bloodworth-Thomason countered, "I care as much about what Delta weighs as I care about seeing Roseanne Barr's tattoo in person.") Burke finally bailed after the fifth season, but the backstage battle only seemed to juice up her characterization. "Delta's abilities as an actress just blossomed," recalled costar Jean Smart. "Suzanne's walk became a swagger," agreed Burke. "Her voice changed, her attitude changed. She became a great broad, and funnier." The same brio informed her short-lived sitcoms *Delta* and *Women of the House,* before Burke left town for New Orleans with her actor husband, Gerald McRaney (*Major Dad*). She started a clothing line for plus-size women and penned her biography, *Delta Style: Eve Wasn't a Size 6 and Neither Am I.* It was five years before she returned for another smart-mouthed, short-lived starring role as the First Lady in *DAG*. "You gotta keep growing," she once philosophized of her up-and-down career, "because then I'll be a fascinating old lady."

TONY DANZA

Born: April 21, 1951

HOUSEHOLD HUNK Tony Danza as a housekeeper? "It worked because he was a tough guy," said *Who's the Boss?* cocreator Martin Cohan of the former boxer. "It made him seem more eccentric when he vacuumed the drapes." With his disarming grin and lovable-lunk persona, Danza cleaned up in the ratings playing the maid to a high-strung suburban businesswoman (Judith Light). The character was, he said, "kind of like me in a good mood." Both were what he called "dese, dem and dose" guys from Brooklyn, and Danza recalls never being allowed out of the house till chores were done. A one-time Golden Gloves contender, Danza fell into acting by accident after being spotted in a gym by a producer of *Taxi.* ("I keep waiting for somebody to say, 'Hey, we're kidding,'" he admitted at the time, but he was a fixture with Sunshine Cab for five seasons.) On *Boss,* the old-school *paesano* traded light double entendres with Light and Katherine Helmond, but made sure to create a G-rated set for his young castmates and would proudly post their report cards. "He was very fatherlike," recalled Danny Pintauro. Danza has two daughters with Tracy, his wife of 17 years, as well as a son from an earlier marriage. *Boss* ended in 1992, but Danza stayed in demand except for a year on the sidelines following a horrific 1993 skiing accident that left him with two broken vertebrae, six crushed ribs, a dislocated leg and a collapsed lung. (After he recovered, he carved a message in the tree he had hit: "T.D. was here—hard.") His two subsequent starring series, *Hudson Street* and *The Tony Danza Show,* both failed, but he got an Emmy nomination for a recurring role on *The Practice.* Most remarkably, he won admiring notices for serious roles on Broadway in *A View from the Bridge* and *The Iceman Cometh.* He also put together a well-received cabaret act, mixing song, tap dance and comedy. "It's every Italian's dream—a microphone, a tuxedo and a stool," he explained. Besides, "Tony spelled backwards is y-not? Look at it this way. For what I do, I ain't bad!"

BAR BELLE As prissy, overeducated barmaid Diane Chambers, Shelley Long drove the *Cheers* crowd nuts with her precise grammar and uptight coquetry. "Every time you ask her a question, you get a paragraph," Long said of her nettlesome character. Still, for five years Diane's tumultuous romance with aging baseball stud Sam Malone (Ted Danson) proved irresistible, winning Long an Emmy and propelling the NBC series into the Top 10. In 1987, when she abruptly quit the show to make films (the script had Diane stranding Sam at the altar for the sake of a juicy book deal), Long provoked a wave of rancor among her colleagues. "I guess they felt I abandoned them and put them in jeopardy," she said. In fact, *Cheers* went on for six years without her, climbing in the ratings from No. 3 to No. 1. Long, on the other hand, was less successful. Her first post-*Cheers* movie, the hit *Outrageous Fortune*, was followed by a string of disappointments and a pair of failed TV sitcoms (CBS's *Good Advice* and The WB's *Kelly Kelly*). Although she was often confused with pretentious academic Diane, the Fort Wayne, Indiana, native was actually a college dropout who developed her comedian's chops with Chicago's Second City troupe. Her second marriage, to investment adviser Bruce Tyson, has lasted 22 years and brought her daughter Juliana. As for the sitcom that established her, Long is grateful that her vocabulary "increased tremendously" and that despite lingering tensions, she was invited back for last call on the *Cheers* '93 sign-off.

SHELLEY LONG

Born: August 23, 1949

SHERMAN HEMSLEY

Born: February 1, 1938

BUNKER MENTALITY "We're movin' on up to the East Side. . . . We finally got a piece of the pie-ie-ie. . . ." The theme song said it loud and proud. In 1975, *The Jeffersons* showcased an upscale black sitcom family nearly a decade before *The Cosby Show.* Feisty Sherman Hemsley drove the popular series as irascible dry-cleaning entrepreneur George Jefferson. Originally a scene-stealer on *All in the Family,* tormenting Archie Bunker with lines like "Pin the tail on the honky," George broke ground for middle-class African-Americans when he and wife "Weezie" (Isabel Sanford) moved on up into a deluxe Manhattan high-rise in the spin-off. "He's a black buffoon," observed actor Robert Hooks. "Still, I love him. He's the only TV image we've got." A kinetic 5'6" corner kid from South Philly, Hemsley escaped to the Air Force and then worked for the post office. "There were fewer murders when I was there," he quipped. He began acting at night and in 1973 caught the eye of *All in the Family* producer Norman Lear. After *The Jeffersons'* 10-year run, Hemsley returned as another short-fused know-it-all, Deacon Frye, on the NBC sitcom *Amen.* A bachelor, he found himself movin' on down to bankruptcy in 1999, but two years later cashed in on his bombastic character in commercials for Old Navy and Denny's. "I used to try and tell folks that I, Sherman Hemsley, am not George, that we have little in common," he said. "But they get such a kick out of it that I usually don't bother."

CYBILL SHEPHERD

Born: February 18, 1950

HAPPY VAMPER It was a modest midseason replacement that blossomed into a prototype for hip, risqué TV. The innuendo-laden banter between *Moonlighting*'s Maddie Hayes (Cybill Shepherd) and David Addison (then unknown Bruce Willis) launched his career and revived hers. Surviving the flameout of a promising start in film (*The Last Picture Show, Taxi Driver*), the former model was suddenly heralded as a Carole Lombard for the '80s, successfully melding beauty and wit. "Maddie is a million miles away from the ice bitches I tend to play," said the Memphis belle. "I'm finally funny." Despite their well-publicized differences, even Willis admitted he and Shepherd made beautiful music together: "When we were 'on,' we hit some notes that will never be played again." But when they were off, they were horrid, and in 1989 the ABC series self-destructed after four seasons, a victim of warring egos, delayed scripts and Shepherd's difficult pregnancy (with twins). She had another explanation. "They made Maddie an unreasonable, hysterical woman," said Shepherd, "because Bruce Willis didn't want to play a jerk anymore. He was too smart and too successful. So where are you going to get the conflict? From Maddie." A year later, Shepherd, a mother of three, went through her second divorce. But proving there are indeed second—and third—acts in America, she came roaring back in 1995, executive-producing and starring in *Cybill*. "She's always thought she's going to have a much longer-lasting career being funny than being the eternal sex goddess," said longtime friend and retired L'Oréal exec James Viera. The CBS comedy let her be both. "I wanted to deal honestly with a woman character who's in her prime—sexually and in every other way," she said. In three years, though, *Cybill* too was canceled. Down but never out, Shepherd went on to host a talk show (the blink-and-you-missed-it *Men Are from Mars, Women Are from Venus*), write a tell-all memoir (*Cybill Disobedience*) and star in NBC's Martha Stewart biopic. Her philosophy? "To me the ultimate sin in life is to be boring," she observed. "I don't play it safe."

FRAN DRESCHER

Born: September 30, 1957

FINE WHINE With the intensity of a jackhammer and the pitch of an upset mallard, her laugh will go down as one of the silliest in history. Sure, Fran Drescher was not the actress you'd cast as Anna Karenina, but as a sitcom star she was perfect. "I'm not Meryl Streep," she said herself. "I'm a pretty girl with a funny voice. It's an odd combination, but that's the package." If it weren't for a fortunate seat upgrade in 1992, it's a package that might never have been delivered. On a flight to Paris, Drescher, noted for her film debut in *Saturday Night Fever* (and her question to John Travolta about whether he was "as good in bed as you are on the dance floor"), was seated in first class next to Jeff Sagansky, then the CBS entertainment president. Before the plane landed, she'd piqued his interest in her idea for a show, and the next year, it was on the air. *The Nanny,* which she coproduced with her then husband, Peter Marc Jacobson, starred Drescher as a cosmetics saleswoman from Queens who happens upon a job minding the three children of a widowed British-born Broadway producer (played by Charles Shaughnessy). "The heartland just loved that little Jewish girl in the short skirts," noted Drescher (if she had to say so herself). Agreed CBS exec Leslie Moonves: "There's something about Fran that is every underdog in America." Before the show was canceled in '99, Drescher and Jacobson split, but they have remained friends, having endured so much together. In '85, two men had broken into their Los Angeles apartment. They tied and gagged Jacobson, and one robbed their home while the other raped both Drescher and a visiting friend. Another tragedy befell her in 2000, when she was diagnosed with uterine cancer and had to undergo a radical hysterectomy. Last year she wrote a book about the experience and the lack of recurrence so far, titled *Cancer Schmancer.* Although Drescher hasn't got a new show in the works yet, there's still the glow of the last one. "I'm like the little engine that could—and did," she said. "I think you just have to have a lot of chutzpah in this life."

Born: September 17, 1948

JOHN RITTER

COMPANY MAN The recipe for *Three's Company* called for one part double entendre to three parts jiggle factor, but somehow the comedic talents of John Ritter bubbled to the top. "John did it perfectly, turning sex into a soufflé," said coproducer Michael Ross. The cooking metaphor is apt: Ritter played a voraciously heterosexual chef who, seeking to room with two hot dishes (Joyce DeWitt and Suzanne Somers), pretended to be gay to outwit a prudish landlord. "John's all about not taking life too seriously," said DeWitt. "There were days we went home from rehearsal with our cheeks sore from laughing." That was a 180 from his earlier series role as Reverend Fordwick on *The Waltons*. As the Hollywood-born son of western great Tex Ritter, he wasn't used to having the spotlight to himself. "Me a TV star?" he once marveled. "I've got to be the luckiest guy in the world." In 1984, *Company* was canceled after seven years, and within a year, so was its spin-off *Three's a Crowd*. But Ritter was snapped up for *Hooperman* and subsequently *Hearts Afire*. He also enjoyed some success in films and guest-starred on everything from *Felicity* to *Ally McBeal* before landing his current series, *8 Simple Rules for Dating My Teenage Daughter*, in 2002. "Twenty-five years ago he played a bachelor," said its creator, Tracy Gamble. "This is like karma coming back to get him." Ritter, a Los Angeles father of four (one with current wife Amy Yasbeck), knows about karma. "If I found a cure for a huge disease," he said, "while I was hobbling up onstage to accept the Nobel Prize they'd be playing the theme song from *Three's Company*."

LISA KUDROW

Born: July 30, 1963

DUMB LIKE A FOX At Vassar, Lisa Kudrow planned to become a doctor, she once said, "or something that indicated that I was a smart person." But she hit the heights flying in the face of that plan, playing two of the ditziest women on TV. First she was Ursula, the spacey waitress on *Mad About You* who once asked star Paul Reiser if he'd like cheese on his cheeseburger. Then, in 1994, she landed the role of Phoebe Buffay, *Friends'* flaky New Age masseuse who croons, "Smelly cat, smelly cat/ What are they feeding you?" When she is in character, Kudrow has said, "people talk slower to me, like I was a 10-year-old." So why isn't she peering through a microscope instead of poring over scripts? She ultimately decided she didn't want to end up like some of her "pompous profs" who "sit around and theorize." Besides, her ambition to follow her father, Lee, an M.D. specializing in headache research (mom Nedra is a travel agent), cooled when she tackled organic chemistry. After graduating in sociobiology, Kudrow moved back to her native L.A., where her brother's childhood pal, comic Jon Lovitz, inspired her to enroll in the Groundlings improv school. Eighteen years later she earns $1 million per episode on *Friends* and has accrued six Emmy nominations and one win. She has been married for eight years to French advertising executive Michel Stern and has a son, Julian. While still fond of playing airheads ("Life's a lot easier when you're dumb"), Kudrow has also earned raves for weightier roles in the films *Analyze This* and *The Opposite of Sex*. "She's like the best kind of jazz there is," said her *Hanging Up* costar Meg Ryan. "You don't know what note she's going to hit, and it's always a surprise."

SMOOTH OPERATOR As Sam Malone, the breezily egotistical, perpetually horny ex-Red Sox relief pitcher who owned Cheers, everybody's favorite Boston watering hole, Ted Danson kept regulars Norm and Cliff—and 35 million viewers—coming back for 11 seasons of gimlet-eyed wisecracks, straight up, no chaser. "I would have been this sweet, sensitive guy until I died if I hadn't played Sam Malone," said the easygoing two-time Emmy winner and ardent environmentalist. In retrospect, he said, "I had no idea how lucky I was to be part of that show—I had a free ride." His costars, a cast of splendidly played eccentrics, dismissed that excessive modesty. "He's the hub of the wheel," declared Woody Harrelson, and Danson became the highest paid TV star of that time. "Ted keeps everyone's sanity," agreed John Ratzenberger. "He absorbs the angst." The father of two had some of his own to deal with, including a 1993 divorce and a film career that peaked back in 1987 with *Three Men and a Baby*. On the set of one flop, *Pontiac Moon,* he met actress Mary Steenburgen. They wed in 1995 and shared a failed sitcom, *Ink,* before Danson returned to prime time on his own in 1998 as *Becker,* a cynical, crankily disillusioned doctor. "It's fun to play someone in his 50s who's grumpy and slightly pissed off," he explained. "I think Sam Malone would have gotten that way eventually, too."

TED DANSON

Born: December 29, 1947

THEY STARTED IN STAND-UP

THEY KILLED (AND SOME NIGHTS DIED) ON THE CLUB CIRCUIT, THE CRUELEST VENUE THIS SIDE OF THE BULLRING—BERNIE MAC DID 25 LONG YEARS, RAY ROMANO 13, ROSEANNE 8—BEFORE CASHING IN WITH THE CUSHIER WORLD OF TV

EDDIE MURPHY

Born: April 3, 1961

THE SKETCH ARTIST Eddie Murphy was on *Saturday Night Live* for just four seasons but left an indelible mark with characters like his cantankerous, cigar-chomping Gumby, his ghetto version of Mr. Rogers and his dead-on Buckwheat update. When he arrived on *SNL* in 1980, he "blew all of us away," said colleague Joe Piscopo. Murphy was still only 19 and fresh from the club circuit on his native Long Island (and a day job as a shoe store clerk). Two years later, he catapulted to movie stardom in *48 Hrs* and then mopped up with smashes like *Trading Places, Beverly Hills Cop* and *Raw,* a film of his acidulous stand-up act. His career cooled with some bombs in the early '90s. "Every bad decision I've made has been based on money," he admitted. "I grew up in the projects, and you don't turn down money there." In 1999 he co-created and voiced the lead character of the FOX animated series *The PJs*. He was also discovering his PG possibilities with films like *The Nutty Professor, Dr. Dolittle* and *Daddy Day Care,* as he settled in suburban New Jersey with his wife, Nicole, and their five children. "When I was young, I knew this was a gift from God," he once said. "I knew there was a reason I was here: to make people laugh."

BOB NEWHART

Born: September 5, 1929

BUTTON-DOWN MIND Bob Newhart's funniest moments have always derived more from the arched eyebrow than the arch comeback. Whether he played a shrink, an innkeeper or a cartoonist (on *The Bob Newhart Show, Newhart* and *Bob,* respectively), his persona was the same: the incredulous everyman around whom lunacy swirled. "He's like the last sane man in an insane world," said *Newhart* castmate John Voldstad (one of the show's two mute Darryl brothers). A mild-mannered former Chicago accountant, Newhart started off doing sketches on '50s radio. He often was at his best on the phone—making imaginary calls to Sir Walter Raleigh, Abraham Lincoln and other historical figures. Those wry one-sided conversations helped propel his breakout 1960 comedy album, *The Button-Down Mind of Bob Newhart,* to No. 1 on the charts. He would reprise his phone shtick as a meek Army private in *Hell Is for Heroes,* his 1962 film debut, and further hone his milquetoast image as Major Major in *Catch-22.* But his greatest triumphs came on TV, first as the *Newhart Show*'s Dr. Bob Hartley in the '70s and then as *Newhart*'s Dick Loudon in the '80s. Tired of playing "the nice guy," he opted to portray *Bob*'s artist Bob McKay as "petty, angry and petulant. It's fun," he said. Not for viewers: *Bob,* launched in '92, lasted little more than a season. That soured Newhart on series TV. Now the septuagenarian father of four grown children with Ginnie, his wife of 39 years, still performs in concerts around the country—despite his fear of flying. "I'm probably not gonna die in a plane crash," he mused last year. "I'll hopefully at 85 get shot by a jealous husband. That's my aim in life now."

FAMILY MAN During his 13 years on the comedy circuit, Ray Romano built his act on stories about his relatives. On his hit CBS sitcom *Everybody Loves Raymond,* art doesn't imitate life so much as plagiarize it. "Very rarely does a funny joke come to me that hasn't happened to me first," he said. When *Raymond* debuted in 1996, the similarities between Ray Romano and Ray Barone were uncanny: Both were married with three children (Romano now has a fourth), both had a policeman brother, and both had slightly kooky parents living nearby. No hard feelings in the Romano clan, though. "If he can benefit by what we do, that's fine," said his father, Albert, a part-time real estate broker. "I do mention to him occasionally that it would be nice to see a few dollars from all this." The family banter in the show is similarly sarcastic. "When we talk, it all sounds real," said Romano. "That appeals to the audience, makes them feel like they're watching real people—dysfunctional but real people." It was Mr. Irony himself, David Letterman, who launched *Raymond* after a *Late Show* appearance convinced him that the New Yawk guy could headline a sitcom. Now decamped to L.A. with his wife of 16 years, Anna, and kids, Romano already has a plan for life after *Raymond.* "I'd like to write a movie. I'd like to get back to stand-up," he said. "You definitely won't find me sitting around eating Oreos."

RAY ROMANO

Born: December 21, 1957

ROBIN WILLIAMS

Born: July 21, 1951

MADMAN FOR ALL SEASONS With just one nonsensical catchphrase—"Nanu-nanu"—Robin Williams beamed himself into prime time in 1978 as Mork, the spaced-out spaceman from Planet Ork. What began as a brilliant one-shot cameo on *Happy Days* quickly morphed into the hit series *Mork & Mindy,* with Pam Dawber as Williams's wholesome straight woman. Kids had a new lunchbox hero, but—this being a family show—they and their parents were spared the topical, sweaty, scatological, stream-of-consciousness patter with which Williams, still in his 20s, had already transformed stand-up comedy. A Juilliard-trained actor whose roommate had been Christopher Reeve, he never did a second series. Instead Williams vaulted to the big screen, with his squinty "blow me down" embodiment of Popeye followed by the title role in *The World According to Garp* and his Oscar-nominated turn in *Good Morning, Vietnam.* (He finally won the statuette in 1997 for his supporting role as a psychiatrist in *Good Will Hunting.*) Always on the prowl for dramatic parts, Williams, who has three children, two with second wife Marsha, has lately surprised audiences, playing creepy villains in *Death to Smoochy, Insomnia* and *One Hour Photo.* But you can't keep a zany man down, as his 2002 nationwide stand-up tour (culminating with a live HBO special) attests. "You're in the center of the hurricane," he said of his act. "It seems like it's going a mile a minute, but you're in control."

JANE CURTIN

Born: September 6, 1947

PRIME TIME PERENNIAL Jane Curtin was one of *Saturday Night Live*'s originals in 1975, perhaps the least flamboyant of the bunch but the most steadily working since. Among her memorable creations were Prymaat Conehead and the "Weekend Update" coanchor whom Dan Aykroyd addressed as "Jane, you ignorant slut." "It was simply the best job I ever had," Curtin recalled of her five years on *SNL*. "Parts of the job were sheer joy." Then she added, "Parts, a nightmare." By '84 she returned as a single mom in *Kate & Allie,* winning back-to-back Emmys and the affection of costars. "There was always clowning around, and Jane was the biggest instigator," said Allison Smith. Finally, Curtin tapped her Conehead past for a 5½-year run on the alien comedy *3rd Rock from the Sun.* "There's really no formula to this; you just get lucky," explained the wife since 1975 of producer Patrick Lynch (they have a daughter). "I keep trying to tell friends in New York who are theater people and movie people what it's like to do a sitcom. I paint a very rosy picture. I don't know that they believe me."

Born: October 5, 1957

BERNIE MAC

GRUFF LOVE Ward Cleaver he's not. Never before has a TV dad barked, "I'm gonna bust your head till the white meat shows." Bernie Mac's brash threats are the 21st-century version of Jackie Gleason's "To the moon, Alice." He is a father figure for a new time, and *The Bernie Mac Show* won a prestigious Peabody Award in 2001, its first season. Loosely echoing his own life (he took in a teenage niece and her daughter), Mac plays a comic turned reluctant guardian of two nieces and a nephew. "Bernie's got an instant appeal that's universal," said Carl Reiner, a costar in *Ocean's Eleven.* "He speaks the truth about life, about families, about kids, and he draws you in with his big heart." A Chicagoan who still lives there with wife Rhonda (they have a daughter), Mac drove a Wonder Bread truck before touring 25 grinding years with an act flavorfully captured on film in *The Original Kings of Comedy.* Mac always said that he was too "aggressive" for TV, and ABC rejected his show before it caught on at FOX. "I appreciate everything I've had," he said, even before he took over the Bill Murray role in the *Charlie's Angels: Full Throttle* sequel. "If it all stopped today, I'd still be proud. I'd still be happy."

BILLY CRYSTAL

Born: March 14, 1948

MR. SHOW-BUSY To paraphrase his Fernando character from *Saturday Night Live,* Billy Crystal still "looks . . . *mah*velous!" And let us tell you why, dahlinks: The acerbic comic, who grew up doing impressions of relatives at home in Long Beach, New York, had showbiz in his blood. (His dad managed Manhattan's Commodore jazz record shop, and Billie Holiday was his babysitter.) After eight years on the stand-up circuit, Crystal made his series debut as Jodie Dallas on *Soap* (1977-81), one of TV's first openly gay characters. ("Women find Jodie very sexy," he once said. "They think they can change him in one night.") Yet it wasn't until his 1984-85 stint on *SNL*—"the best year of my career"—that Crystal emerged as a star, mimicking Muhammad Ali, Howard Cosell and Sammy Davis Jr. (for whom he used to open in clubs) and creating originals like egotistical borscht-belt comic Buddy Young Jr. He enjoyed his biggest nights on TV, however, as the Emmy-winning seven-time emcee of the Oscars. Crystal's own forays into film include *When Harry Met Sally . . . , City Slickers* ("I wanted to make *Deliverance* with laughs") and *Analyze This* and its sequel. Still, his heart belongs to stand-up. "I've accomplished so many things," said Crystal, who has two daughters with Janice, his wife of 33 years, "but there's nothing like having an audience going nuts." It just feels *mah*velous.

DOMESTIC GODZILLA On *The Tonight Show* in 1983, after eight years toiling out of that comedy mecca of Denver, Roseanne Barr went national with a caustic brand of housewife humor that was equal parts Phyllis Diller and Sam Kinison. It did not seem ready for prime time, but in 1988, ABC unleashed *Roseanne,* a family sitcom headed by a mom who was about as close to Donna Reed as a hyena is to a kitten. "There was nothing on the air that showed the difficulty and the wonderful aspects [of being a working mother]," said co-executive producer Marcy Carsey. A curmudgeon with a caramel center, Roseanne Conner bowled, told her kids to play in traffic and traded loving insults with her husband (John Goodman)—all in an effort, said Barr, "to redefine the role of women in television and the media and society." The Utah-born comedian won an Emmy and kept the series going nine years, while running a simultaneous tabloid freak show with plastic surgeries, weight-loss battles, charges of abuse against her parents, a volatile marriage to Tom Arnold, a claim of multiple personalities and, of course, the crotch-grabbing national anthem debacle. "I don't choose the negative attention, despite what people think," she said. "I sometimes get what I think is a good idea, but my judgment is wrong." The thrice-divorced mother of five remained in the L.A. area, weathered the failure of a syndicated talk show and returned to the fray with an ABC reality series. "I'm a comic, and I'm supposed to outrage and make people laugh," Roseanne once said. "Part of makin' people laugh is to shake up their thinkin'. That's what I came here to do."

ROSEANNE

Born: November 3, 1952

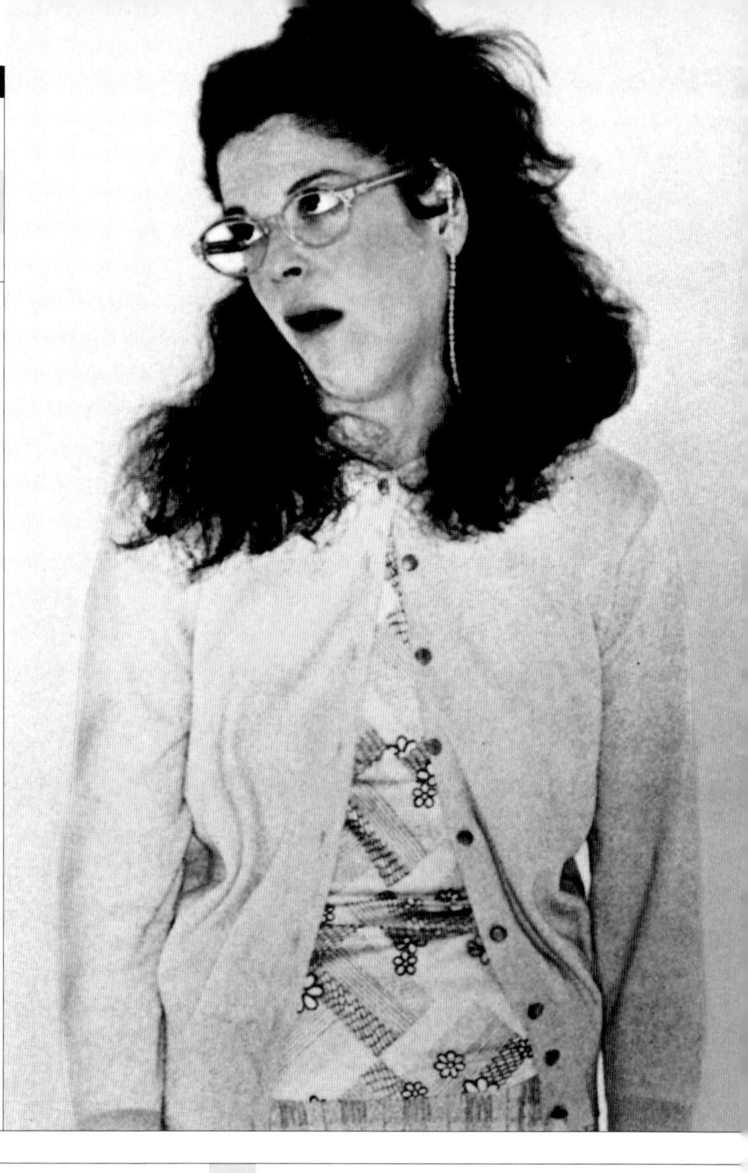

GILDA RADNER

Born: June 28, 1946 Died: May 20, 1989

SATURDAY NIGHT LOVE As sassy Roseanne Roseannadanna, she obsessed over earwax and hair on the soap. Her hearing-impaired Emily Litella debated "violins on TV." And as nerdy teenager Lisa Loopner (right), she was forever dodging "noogies." Like her characterizations during five seasons on NBC's *Saturday Night Live,* Gilda Radner was bighearted and unabashedly vulnerable. "You felt like you knew her," said writer Alan Zweibel. "She was a star, but she was your sister." Daughter of a wealthy Detroit family, she attended the University of Michigan before joining Toronto's Second City troupe and impressing *SNL* producer Lorne Michaels. In 1981, Radner said, her "life went from black and white to Technicolor" when she met husband-to-be Gene Wilder on the set of *Hanky Panky.* But their happiness was short-lived. Diagnosed with ovarian cancer in 1986, Radner fought tenaciously, retaining her humor until the end. "My life had made me funny, and cancer wasn't going to change that," she wrote in her book *It's Always Something.* When she died at 42, a generation felt it had lost a friend. "She had this need to be loved by everyone," said Wilder. "And she was."

Born: June 13, 1953

TIM ALLEN

DOOFUS DAD As Tim "The Tool Man" Taylor, the blithely bumbling Mr. Fixit cable-show host, Tim Allen was famous for his macho mantra "More power!" which just supercharged the mayhem on the set—and the ratings of ABC's *Home Improvement.* At home, the Tool Man reigned—or thought he did—as a clueless suburban husband and father of three boisterous boys. Allen had developed the character from his "Men Are Pigs" stand-up persona ("When I walk into that [Sears] Craftsman tool department, my nipples get rock-hard!"). Allen's life before and after the smash Disney sitcom was a roller coaster. Busted for selling cocaine in '79, he served 28 months in prison, then toiled for an ad agency while moonlighting in comedy clubs. Mellowed by TV, Allen's wit translated into hit films in the mid-'90s like *The Santa Clause* and *Toy Story* (as the voice of pompous space cadet Buzz Lightyear). In 1997, while earning a then-record $1.25 million an episode for *Home,* he was pulled over for drunk driving near his home in suburban Detroit. A stint in alcohol rehab proved successful. "I was able to take control," he said last year. "I no longer drink." But his marriage to college sweetheart Laura Deibel ended in 1999 (they have a daughter, Kady). His sitcom was finally finished that same year but not his days as a pop caricature—or caricature pop. Allen has signed to do the big-screen version of *Father Knows Best.* More power to him.

DYNASTY DUDE Taking on the mantle of Bill Cosby, Damon Wayans got down and got funky in 2001 when, as co-executive producer and star of ABC's *My Wife & Kids,* he revived the black family sitcom. As Michael Kyle, the prosperous owner of a delivery-truck company, Wayans delivers zingers to his stockbroker wife and their three children, who are quick to sass him back. The Cosby comparison doesn't faze Wayans. "We are doing a family show about my family life," said the comic actor, who, with former wife Lisa, has four kids. (Eldest son Damon Jr. is his assistant on the set; daughter Cara has a recurring role.) "Who knows me better than my family?" Well, how about the *rest* of his family (nine siblings, including Keenan, Marlon, Shawn and Kim)? In the '90s, the Wayanses, led by Keenan, pushed the envelope of TV humor as far as FOX would allow with their bawdy, brash '90s revue *In Living Color.* Damon had been a major player on that show, specializing in over-the-top characters like a campily gay film critic and a disabled handyman. The latter drew particularly harsh criticism for being insensitive, but Wayans knew whereof he spoofed. Born with a clubfoot and forced to wear leg braces as a child in New York City, he deflected insults from other kids by humorously pointing out their own flaws and foibles. "It made me an observer with a running commentary," he said—perfect training for stand-up. In 1984, after just two years on the circuit, Wayans landed a bit part in Eddie Murphy's *Beverly Hills Cop.* He soon found steady work in other films, but it was his exposure on *Color* that won him top billing in '90s movies like *Mo' Money* (with Marlon), *Major Payne* and *Blankman.* Now, as a TV paterfamilias, he says he has finally grown up: "It's hard to act like a fool with a suit on."

DAMON WAYANS

Born: September 4, 1960

BEFORE THEY WERE MOVIE STARS

The road to the Hollywood walk of fame is often a humbling scramble through the bramble of series TV. Would you believe that George Clooney survived 15 failed pilots, that Hilary Swank got canned by Aaron Spelling and that Meg Ryan and at least two other major leading ladies sprang from *As the World Turns*?

HALLE BERRY

Originally a model herself, she made her acting debut as an aspiring catwalker (with Michael Learned and Leah Remini, hugging, and Alison Elliott, right) in an '89 sitcom. Titled *Living Dolls,* it died in three months.

BEN AFFLECK

At 21, he passed for a 16-year-old high school football star in *Against the Grain*, a 1993-94 small-town drama set in Texas.

DENZEL WASHINGTON

Before he set hearts aflutter, he mended them as an insecure doctor on *St. Elsewhere.* In 1989, a year after the gritty hospital drama ended, Washington won the first of his two Oscars.

JULIANNE MOORE

For three years she played the good-and-evil twins Frannie and Sabrina on *As the World Turns* (here, with Steve Bassett) and in 1988 collected a Daytime Emmy.

QUEEN LATIFAH

The rapper-turned-actress headlined the sitcom *Living Single* (with Kim Coles, left) from 1993 to 1998. She also wrote and performed the theme, and in 1999 hosted her own syndicated talk show.

GEORGE CLOONEY

Talk about doggedness and paying dues! En route to *ER*, he shot 15 failed pilots and toiled in six different series including (above, with Mindy Cohn) *The Facts of Life* in '85.

MEG RYAN

In *As the World Turns* (with Frank Runyeon, left, and Scott Bryce in '82), she hung in for two years as a hapless girl-next-door caught in a sordid love triangle.

JOHNNY DEPP

A school dropout and garage musician, Depp (with Peter DeLuise, right) finally jump-started his acting career in '87 as an amiable, baby-faced undercover cop on *21 Jump Street.*

MICHELLE PFEIFFER

At 20, she was aptly cast as "The Bombshell" in 1979's *Delta House,* a toned-down-for-TV version of the raunchy movie smash *Animal House.* After its 13-episode life span, Pfeiffer (right) went on to star in *B.A.D. Cats,* a six-week dog.

LEONARDO DiCAPRIO

In 1991, six years before he was famously boatless, he portrayed a homeless child taken in by the family of a suburban shrink on *Growing Pains*.

MARISA TOMEI

Yet another vet of the *As the World Turns* boot camp, Tomei advanced to prime time as a flighty, callow and annoyingly loquacious coed on *A Different World*, a 1987 *Cosby Show* spin-off.

TOM HANKS

The '80s drag comedy *Bosom Buddies* gave America a preview of Hanks's limitless range. He (and fellow ad-guy roomie Peter Scolari, left) cross-dressed to live in a low-rent, women-only residence.

JIM CARREY

The comic was a fledgling cartoonist in 1984's *The Duck Factory.* It got shot down in three months, but Carrey found series success six years later on the sketch show *In Living Color,* creating memorable characters like Fire Marshall Bill.

HELEN HUNT

She played in no less than five series by age 20—among them the 1974 cop drama *Amy Prentiss* (with Jessica Walter, right)—before her TV superstardom as Paul Reiser's cynical better half on *Mad About You*.

DEMI MOORE

Following a brief modeling career, she was encouraged to try acting by her neighbor Nastassja Kinski. She debuted in '82, as an investigative reporter (here, with Tristan Rogers) on the soap *General Hospital*.

EDDIE GRIFFIN

On *Malcolm & Eddie*—a hip, urban take on *The Odd Couple*—Griffin proved the perfect comic foil to sitcom vet Malcolm-Jamal Warner (left). The show, which aired from 1996 to 2000, helped establish the newby UPN network.

KIM BASINGER

After a guest gig on *Starsky and Hutch* in 1976, she landed her own cop show the following year, playing an adorable rookie (opposite Lou Antonio) on *Dog and Cat*. It was put down, alas, after a mere three months.

HILARY SWANK

In 1998, she was informed by *Beverly Hills, 90210* producer Aaron Spelling that her part as the love interest of Ian Ziering (above) was "not working." The axing, however devastating, made Swank available months later for her Oscar-winning breakthrough in *Boys Don't Cry*.

JADA PINKETT SMITH

The comedy *A Different World* launched Pinkett (left) in 1991. She played a sassy, street-smart college student (opposite, from left, Charnele Brown, Lou Myers and Kadeem Hardison).

BILLY BOB THORNTON

His maiden series, 1989's *The Outsiders,* was canceled in its fifth month, but Thornton rebounded as a character named Billy Bob in 1992 for a three-season run on *Hearts Afire,* a sitcom starring the ubiquitous John Ritter (left).

SANDRA BULLOCK

In 1990, before getting up to *Speed,* she played a secretary newly promoted to junior exec (with Anthony Tyler Quinn, left) in *Working Girl,* a short-lived adaptation of the Melanie Griffith feature.

Can You Spot . . .

JENNIFER LOPEZ

With its multicultural cast, in-your-face irreverence and underclad dance troupe called the Fly Girls, *In Living Color* was a groundbreaking series of the '90s, not to mention a star factory. As creator, talent scout and headliner, Keenen Ivory Wayans (C) showcased comers like Jim Carrey and David Alan Grier, and had the pleasure of auditioning the 2,000 Fly Girl contenders. His picks included Cari French (B), Lisa Marie Todd (D), Carrie Ann Inaba (E), Diedre Lang (F) and, yes, Jennifer Lopez (A). J.Lo's one regret from those days: "I wish I had better [looking] pictures."

SALMA HAYEK

A major soap star in Mexico, Salma Hayek headed to Hollywood in '91. Her first recurring role came two years later in a family sitcom, *The Sinbad Show*, with Sinbad himself (B), T.K. Carter (C), Willie Norwood (A) and Erin Davis (E). That's Hayek (D), caught before her part was dropped after just one month.

RYAN PHILLIPPE

Among the legacies of the 35-year-old soap *One Life to Live* are daytime's first openly gay male teen in 1992 and the rookie actor who played him. It was Ryan Phillippe (B), shown with Chris McKenna (A) and Kelly Cheston (C). "I was completely paranoid," said Ryan of accepting the role. "I wasn't sure how my friends and family would handle it."

LUCY LIU

The blue-collar comedy *Pearl*, about a loading-dock manager, Rhea Perlman (E), seeking her college degree, didn't last for a sophomore season. Among the cast: Kevin Corrigan (A), Malcolm McDowell (B), Carol Kane (D) and Lucy Liu (C) as a grade-obsessed classmate.

THEY ARE ONE-OF-A-KIND ORIGINALS: THE BULLDOG INTERVIEWER, THE BRAINY QUIZMASTER, THE LEGGY LETTER TURNER, THE NEIGHBORLY KIDS'-SHOW HOST. . . . EACH OF THEM IS A THREE-DIMENSIONAL FIGURE WHO HAS BROKEN TV'S FOURTH WALL (OR, AS WITH ANARCHIC OZZY OSBOURNE, SHATTERED IT)

STARRING AS THEM

KATIE COURIC

Born: January 7, 1957

MORNING GLORY "Sometimes I feel as if I'm in a made-for-TV movie," said Katie Couric. Her life certainly seems to have the melodramatic elements. When Couric, who had served a brief stint as NBC's Pentagon correspondent, got called to duty as *Today* cohost in 1991 (replacing Deborah Norville), *Washington Post* TV critic Tom Shales hailed her as "the perfect morning companion—assured, natural, gratifyingly unphony." Couric's star shone even brighter after tragedy struck. Her attorney husband, Jay Monahan, with whom she had two daughters, Ellie and Carrie, died of colon cancer in 1998. He was 42. Couric used *Today* as a bully pulpit to advocate early diagnostic testing ("Get your butt to the doctor") and even had her own colonoscopy televised in 2000. Less than two years later, her sister Emily Couric, a state senator in their native Virginia, succumbed at 54 to pancreatic cancer. Meanwhile, the tabloids were tracking Katie's bicoastal romance with sitcom producer Tom Werner (*3rd Rock from the Sun*). Now, with a $13 million-a-year contract, Couric has expanded into prime-time interview specials—and even a May 2003 sweeps swap with *Tonight Show* host Jay Leno. "I'm still ambitious," said Couric. "I want to win. I want to be the first. And you know what? It's that quality that's gotten me where I am."

SELVES

OZZY OSBOURNE

Born: December 3, 1948

BLEEPING SUCCESS If you had told him during his heyday of beheading bats and frequenting rehab that he would eventually be revered as the 21st-century Ozzie Nelson, Ozzy Osbourne would have said, "F--- off!" But no one could have predicted the clamorous success of MTV's reality series *The Osbournes,* chronicling the daily lives of the foulmouthed heavy metaler, his wife/manager, Sharon, and their children Kelly and Jack (elder daughter Aimee declined to participate). Witnessing Osbourne struggle with domestic travails (operating the remote, taking out the trash) not only endeared a nation to the Prince of Darkness but also made him an unlikely dad figure. "I've become everybody's American father, and I'm not even American!" reveled the shock rocker. Born John Michael Osbourne in Birmingham, England, he quit school at 15 and served two months in jail for burglary before cofounding Black Sabbath in the late '60s. But credit his business-savvy spouse for launching Osbourne's lucrative solo career as well as the family TV show, on which he gives his sincerest performance. "All the stuff onstage, the craziness, it's all just a role I play," Osbourne confessed. "I am a family man."

MIKE WALLACE

Born: May 9, 1918

THE GRAND INQUISITOR For more than 30 years the reigning star of CBS's *60 Minutes* has unleashed his bulldog interview style on shifty CEOs, corrupt politicos and sundry other notables. "I've never been afraid to ask an irreverent or confrontational question," said Mike Wallace. "I wanted to know the answers." Grilling everyone from Yasser Arafat to Barbra Streisand, Wallace, said colleague Steve Kroft, has the "ability to ask the question that gets to the center of the issue, the core of the person." Born in suburban Boston, he launched his career with a string of less-auspicious jobs, including radio announcer and game show host, before becoming a CBS News correspondent in 1963. In five years he moved on to what would become the longest-running show on prime-time TV. Twelve Emmys and countless exposés later, Wallace is still at it. "I marvel at Mike," said correspondent Ed Bradley. "What physical and emotional energy!" Though he battled depression in the '80s and early '90s, he recovered with the help of therapy, medication and the support of fourth wife Mary Yates. Now, with homes in New York City and on Martha's Vineyard, the grandfather of 11 is "really happy with my life," he said. "Family. Health. Still working. C'mon, what's not to be happy?"

Born: February 18, 1957

VANNA WHITE

LETTER PERFECT "It all started when I was about 3 and ate a bowl of alphabet soup," joked Vanna White. Twenty-five years later, the former model from South Carolina was wriggling into glitzy gowns, helping contestants play hangman on *Wheel of Fortune* and en route to her own line of dresses, fragrances, dolls and jewelry on the Home Shopping Network. White had been eking out a living in commercials and B movies when she was plucked from 200 Vanna-bes at an audition by *Wheel* producer Merv Griffin, who admired her Rita Hayworth quality and stage ease. "She has to know where the lights are going to pop," he said. "That's a lot to think about—especially in high heels." In the next few years, *Wheel* became the highest-rated show in syndication. Once linked with Sylvester Stallone and Corbin Bernsen, the divorced mother of two lives in Hollywood Hills and marvels at Vannamania. "I think people like me because I'm just a real person," she said. "I'm sincere and not intimidating to anybody."

DAVID LETTERMAN

Born: April 12, 1947

GAP-TOOTHED GENIUS He had been late-night TV's highest-paid defector, bolting NBC for CBS (and a $14 million-a-year contract) in 1993 after losing out to Jay Leno as the heir apparent to Johnny Carson. Though famously cranky and sardonic, David Letterman won our hearts seven years later by thanking onstage the surgeons who'd saved his life with a quintuple bypass. (He also quipped, "A bypass is what happened to me when I didn't get *The Tonight Show.*") But what really secured his status as a pop culture guru was his performance six days after the 9/11 terrorist attacks, when, gingerly yet gracefully, he let a grieving nation—and anxious showbiz peers—know that it was okay to start laughing again. Of course, the Indianapolis-born onetime TV weatherman has always been at his best just being Dave—with his Stupid Pet Tricks, Thrill Cam, Top 10 Lists and silly human stunts (such as dropping watermelons off the top of the Broadway studio where *Late Night* tapes). His other trademark is irreverent banter with guests ranging from an F-word-spouting Madonna to a breast-flashing Drew Barrymore to a spaced-out Farrah Fawcett. His private life, which the once-married comedian shares with his production-company manager Regina Lasko, has received far less exposure—except when he's nailed for speeding, or when a stalker breaks into his home, or when his octogenarian mom, Dorothy, turns up as a guest. Or when Letterman himself fails to show up at all—such as when he was recently sidelined for five weeks with a painful bout of shingles. Away from his familiar desk, he has had mixed success. Though he bombed memorably in his sole stint as Oscars emcee in 1995, as a producer he has spawned such hits as *Ed* and *Everybody Loves Raymond.* Everybody seems to love Dave, too. In 2002—his 20th year in late night—ABC tried to entice him to jump ship once again, but he stayed put at CBS, which agreed to pay him $30 million-plus a year. At any price, Letterman is not for sale. "Dave is always irrepressibly and unavoidably himself," said CBS News anchorman Dan Rather, a frequent guest. "In a copycat world, he is a true original."

NICEST NEIGHBOR For 33 years, it was a beautiful day in the neighborhood. One of TV's landmark figures, genial and gentle-mannered Fred McFeely Rogers spoke frankly and gently to three generations of children. But his playland of make-believe on *Mister Rogers' Neighborhood* was not all Skittles and gumdrops. The Pennsylvania native never sugarcoated childhood's scariest things: divorce, death, loneliness, anger. "Have you ever been so mad you wanted to bite?" he asked. "Whatever is mentionable is manageable," he believed. Although he was an ordained Presbyterian minister who didn't smoke or drink or eat meat, Rogers was no prude. "He was very open-minded," said actor Michael Keaton, once a *Neighborhood* stagehand. "The staff would pull practical jokes, and he loved it." Stubbornly true to his vision of TV as a teaching medium, Rogers, who had two sons of his own with Joanne, his wife of 51 years, garnered 61 Emmy nominations. His careful, slow delivery was often parodied, and he dealt with his feelings about it directly, of course. "It has hurt, because I am who I am," he said. "Nobody likes to be made fun of." The Smithsonian owns one of his zippered cardigans, for he was a national treasure whose shows may well run forever. But Rogers died of cancer in 2003, and the neighborhood will never be the same.

FRED ROGERS

Born: March 20, 1928 Died: February 27, 2003

JAY LENO

Born: April 28, 1950

LEADING WITH HIS CHIN "If I have one advantage, it's that I will try to work harder than the next guy," said Jay Leno. His sweat ethic may explain why, since Leno took over from Carson a decade ago, *The Tonight Show* has remained No. 1 overall in its time slot. No sooner does one hour wrap than TV's hardest working comedian is busy writing jokes for the next. It's their topicality that has made his monologues the most quoted of any comedian's. From the O.J. Simpson case (with the Dancing Itos) to the Monica Lewinsky affair ("the golden age of comedy," said Leno) to the fall of Saddam Hussein, Leno skillfully skewers presidents, CEOs and celebs alike. Longtime rival David Letterman may have more cachet, but it was Leno who got to ask actor Hugh Grant (who had been caught with a prostitute), "What the hell were you thinking?" Married for 23 years to wife Mavis (an outspoken advocate for Afghan women), the comic from suburban New York lives modestly in L.A.—if you don't count his garage full of vintage cars and motorcycles. Leno ain't apologizing. "Most guys," he noted, "have one car and 15 or 16 girlfriends."

Born: July 22, 1940

ALEX TREBEK

QUIZ WHIZ The erudite emcee of *Jeopardy!,* TV's second most popular syndicated show (after *Wheel of Fortune*), Alex Trebek couldn't help himself. Asked whether he would wed this woman—second wife Jean Currivan—at their 1990 nuptials in Los Angeles, Trebek responded, "The answer is . . . yes." Of course, on *Jeopardy!,* which the Canadian-born former newsman began emceeing in 1984, the answers precede the questions. And so will ours. The category: Significant Numbers.

A: 3. Q: How many celebs did Trebek once name as his "dream" contestants? They were Jodie Foster (who has since appeared), Kevin Spacey and Sean Connery.

A: 2. Q: How many philosophy degrees does he hold?

A: 35. Q: How many years did he wear a mustache before shaving it off ("just on a whim") in 2001?

A: 24. Q: How many years separate Trebek and Currivan? "At first it worried me," he said. "But then I thought, The hell with it. We'll make it work." They obviously have: Three weeks after their wedding, Jean was pregnant with son Matthew, who was born in 1991; daughter Emily arrived two years later.

SINGULAR SENSATION A rose is a rose, but Rosie O'Donnell is constantly reinventing herself. From New York-based stand-up comic to Hollywood character actress (*A League of Their Own*) to Broadway diva (Rizzo in *Grease*) to talk show Queen of Nice (*The Rosie O'Donnell Show*) to disgruntled editor of her own magazine (*Rosie,* in whose pages she discussed her battle with depression and a scary hand infection) and back to stand-up, O'Donnell is nothing if not unpredictable. The third of five children of a Long Island homemaker (who died when she was 10) and an electrical engineer (from whom she is estranged), O'Donnell hit her stride as the Emmy-winning daytime doyenne who fawned over A-list guests like Tom Cruise and Barbra Streisand, and dished about her adopted kids Parker, Chelsea and Blake. Of more interest to fans was the arrival in 2002 of Vivienne Rose, conceived through the artificial insemination of her companion, Kelli Carpenter, a former Nickelodeon exec. O'Donnell, who came out as gay last year, has long been a magnet for controversy: sparring with actor and NRA advocate Tom Selleck over gun control; pulling the plug on her show in '02 after six years to focus on her children—then walking away from *Rosie* four months later, after a power struggle with media giant Gruner + Jahr USA (which sued its ex-editor for $100 million; she countersued for $125 million). Win or lose, O'Donnell puts family first: "To be able to have a child who is safe and held and told, 'I love you,' that's my greatest success story."

ROSIE O'DONNELL

Born: March 21, 1962

Born: December 22, 1945

DIANE SAWYER

HEADLINE HUNTER "Before you hear it from someone else," Dan Rather told Diane Sawyer in 1978, "I don't think you should have been hired." Welcome to network news. Sawyer, a former America's Junior Miss and Wellesley grad, arrived at CBS after helping Richard Nixon write his memoirs. "People stopped talking when I walked into the room," she recalled. Over the next two decades, the silence turned to buzz. At CBS and later ABC, the three-time Emmy winner nailed "gets" from Saddam Hussein to Michael Jackson and then-wife Lisa Marie Presley. Since 1999, Sawyer's smooth, reassuring authority has helped make *Good Morning America* a respectable rival of the leading *Today Show.* Sawyer, who once dated Warren Beatty and Henry Kissinger, shares a Manhattan apartment with brainy director husband Mike Nichols (*The Birdcage*). Her pal Candice Bergen calls Sawyer "infinitely smarter than most other kids. A girl of tremendous curiosity and a great sense of adventure." Where will she head next? The vibe says Sawyer might replace anchors Peter Jennings or Rather, but, as then-ABC News boss Roone Arledge said in 1996, "she could be off writing poetry. She has dimensions most people in television don't have."

REGIS PHILBIN

Born: August 25,1931

KAFFEEKLATSCH KING Daytime talkers were looking for fresh gambits in 1988: Phil Donahue did a show in a dress, Sally Jessy Raphaël strolled with hookers, and Oprah dieted away 67 lbs. Then came *Live! with Regis & Kathie Lee.* With an improbable exuberance, Regis Philbin, a former NBC page who was once Joey Bishop's late-night sidekick, and Kathie Lee Gifford, a onetime gospel singer and cruise line pitchwoman, started a revolution by jabbering intimately to each other about their lives. (She once confided that because of an infection, her nipples "went out this far"; he gave a wince-inducing account of his kidney stones.) Wedged between big-time guests like Madonna and Antonio Banderas, their chatter helped *Live!* reach 18 million viewers weekly, and it still babbles along (now with cohost Kelly Ripa). Producer Michael Gelman attributes its staying power to Philbin's "rare ability to be himself on camera. He can look through the lens and connect." In 1999, the Bronx-bred Navy vet, a fervent alumni booster of Notre Dame's Fighting Irish, found another lucrative lifeline: moonlighting as host of *Who Wants to Be a Millionaire.* The game show drew some 26 million viewers, becoming the pop-culture comet of the moment. It reminded Philbin, a father of four who shares Park Avenue digs with Joy, his wife of 33 years, of a lesson he already knew better than most. "Someday," he said, "this will all just be something in a TV trivia book." Oh, Reege.

FROM CHRISSY'S NAUGHTY GIGGLE TO MAGNUM'S EYEBROW WIGGLE TO C.J.'S SWIMSUIT JIGGLE . . . PRIME TIME'S BEAUTIFUL PEOPLE HEATED UP A COOL MEDIUM WITH THEIR PANACHE, PIZZAZZ AND PIERCING BADINAGE

SEXY, SEXY, SEXY

PAMELA ANDERSON

Born: July 1, 1967

VENUS IN SPANDEX There are arguably two good reasons why *Baywatch* became the most-watched show on earth in the '90s, ogled by 1 billion viewers in more than 100 countries: (1) No subtitles required. (2) Pamela Anderson. The syndicated series about L.A. lifeguards showcased the buff bods of its cast—none more curvaceous than that of Anderson, who had risen to fame as a *Playboy* model and as the first "Tool Time Girl" on ABC's *Home Improvement.* As *Baywatch*'s Casey Jean (C.J.) Parker, she did mouth-to-mouth on drowning victims as well as coworkers like Matt (David Charvet, with whom Anderson was briefly involved offscreen). After five seasons C.J. quit to marry a rock star. By odd coincidence, the Canadian-born actress was wed at the time to Mötley Crüe drummer Tommy Lee in a volatile three-year union that steamed up the gossip columns. Divorced in 1998, they continue to share the parenting responsibilities for sons Brandon and Dylan. Now engaged to musician Kid Rock, Anderson most recently starred in the syndicated *V.I.P.* as the full-figured head of a celebrity bodyguard firm. "There are already a lot of serious actors," she said. "I respect these people, but I just want to be the one who has fun."

DAVID DUCHOVNY

Born: August 7, 1960

FOXY FELLOW He was snatched by aliens, swarmed by mutant bugs, slimed by a giant fungus and scorned by his fellow FBI agents (who nicknamed him Spooky). Yet through nine eerie seasons of *The X-Files,* David Duchovny's embattled character Fox Mulder (no relation to the network that carried his show) never lost his soulful-eyed, boyish sense of wonderment over all things paranormal. That—and a '94 episode that showed Mulder in a red Speedo swimsuit—may explain why female fans swooned over the Manhattan-born Princeton grad, a once-aspiring Ph.D. candidate in English at Yale. "All the reasons I had for getting into acting were mercenary," he said. "But once I started classes I realized it was something I could enjoy on a spiritual and emotional level." His minimalist emoting didn't generate much box office in films like *The Rapture, Kalifornia* and *Playing God.* Even the big-screen version of *The X-Files* got mixed reviews. But the series vaulted to Nielsen's Top 10 by its fourth season, due in no small part to the sexual chemistry—and tension—between Mulder and fellow agent Dana Scully (Gillian Anderson), with whom he bonded and flirted and, in the finale, locked lips. "Mulder was driven by intellect," Duchovny explained. "So I had a good instinct on this guy being chaste, and yet all the sex was in his head." (His own cerebral sex appeal inspired Bree Sharp's 1999 pop single "David Duchovny," with its plaintive refrain "Why won't you love me?") Ratings sank, not surprisingly, after Duchovny left in 2000 over a financial dispute with FOX, only to return for a few appearances when the series concluded two years later. By then he was happily wed to actress Téa Leoni (the couple have a daughter and a son). Duchovny has struck out with recent X-tracurricular projects, including the sci-fi spoof *Evolution.* Writing or directing may be in his future. As for his past: "Maybe," he mused playfully, "I'll donate my red Speedo to the Smithsonian. They can stuff it with two plums and a gherkin and put it on display." Now that's spooky.

SARAH JESSICA PARKER

Born: March 25, 1965

COSMO GIRL Playing freewheeling Carrie Bradshaw on HBO's *Sex and the City* is "like having illegal behavior sanctioned," said Sarah Jessica Parker. "I have to sleep with men on the show, and I have to smoke cigarettes on the show, and I have to wear revealing clothes. I'm so lucky." So are fans who become voyeurs as Parker, Kim Cattrall, Kristin Davis and Cynthia Nixon, cast as successful Manhattan career women, compare notes over brunch on the prowess, preferences (tantric sex, anyone?) and shortcomings of their various—and numerous—bed partners. Offscreen, Parker, a native of Cincinnati who played the lead in Broadway's *Annie* and a gawky teen on TV's *Square Pegs,* is "really shy about talking about sex or anything like that," confided a friend. And unlike Carrie, who still carries a torch for Mr. Big (Chris Noth), her on-and-off tycoon lover over the years, Parker has already found her Mr. Right. Previously linked to Robert Downey Jr., Nicolas Cage (her *Honeymoon in Vegas* groom) and the late JFK Jr., she has been wed since 1997 to actor Matthew Broderick (*The Producers*), with whom she has an infant son, James. Amid what she called "hurtful" rumors last year that the match was in trouble, Parker issued a challenge to Barbara Walters: "Come see me in 25, 30 years, when I am still married to the same man."

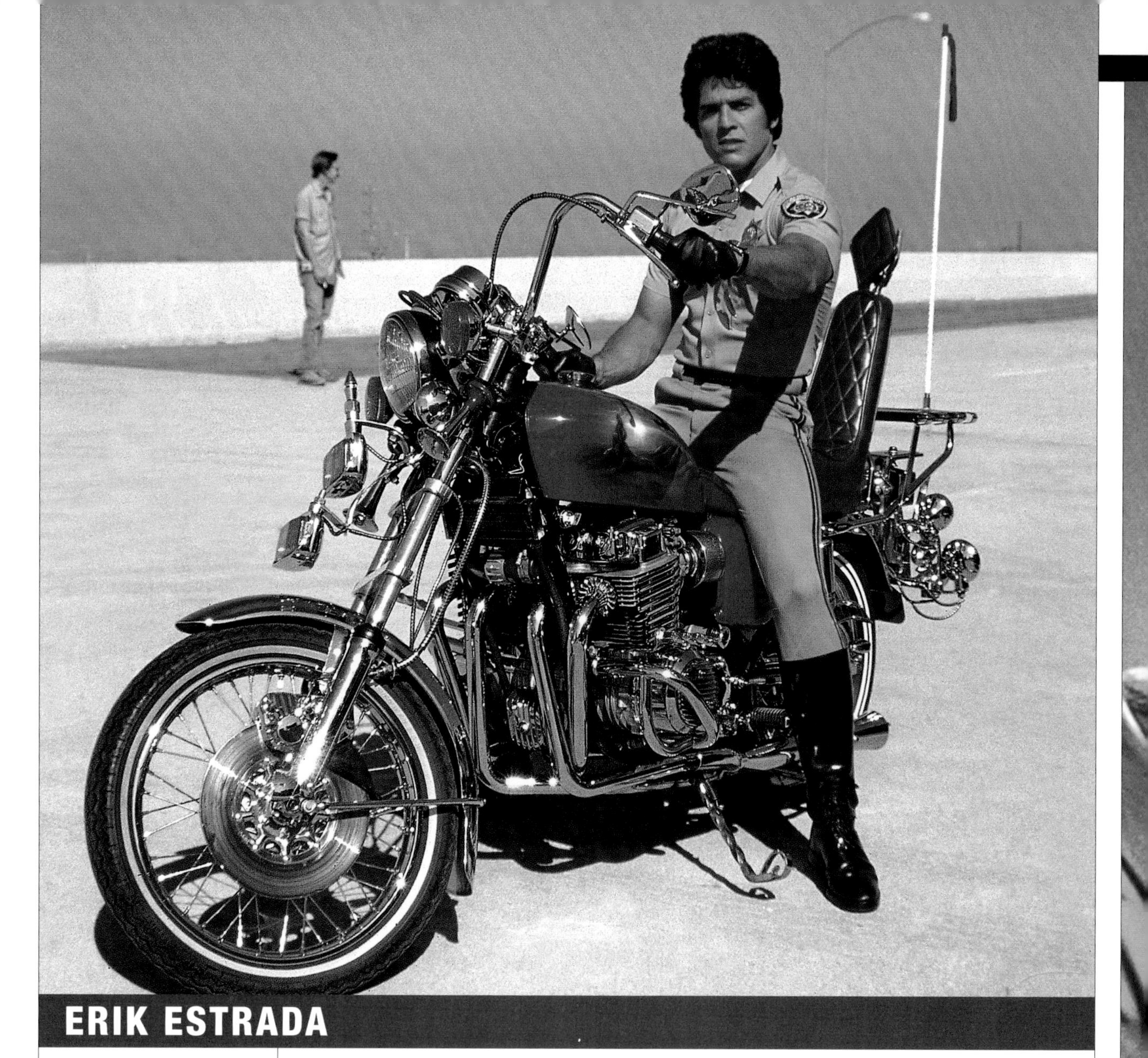

ERIK ESTRADA

Born: March 16, 1949

EASY RIDER As Frank "Ponch" Poncherello on NBC's *CHiPs,* Erik Estrada rode out of nowhere in 1977 and onto the bedroom walls of teenage girls across America. Not since the '50s, when Marlon Brando glowered astride his Triumph in *The Wild One,* had a man and a motorcycle—in Estrada's case, a Kawasaki—seemed so sexy together. *CHiPs* (an acronym for California Highway Patrol) teamed Estrada with Larry Wilcox (as his police partner Jon Baker), but it was Estrada's smoldering good looks and happy-go-lucky demeanor that put fans in hog heaven for six seasons. "It was so much fun for me," said Estrada, "to get on that bike and bust the bad guys and help out the kids. And to get the babes." In real life, Estrada butted helmets with Wilcox, who quit a year before the show ended in 1983. ("We were like two children on the same playground who couldn't get along," Wilcox said.) Earlier Estrada himself had walked out briefly in a salary dispute with the producers. He won a major pay hike and, after being hospitalized for a motorcycle crash on the set, got them to fork over a Rolls-Royce as well. "People may perceive you to be a pain in the ass," he said years later. "But they see that you don't mind being laughed at and laughing at yourself." For a while after *CHiPs,* Estrada didn't have much to smile about, mired in direct-to-video flicks like *The Divine Enforcer* and being seen mostly in celebrity tennis tournaments. Things picked up when he and Wilcox, having patched up their differences, spoofed their *CHiPs* roles for 1993's *National Lampoon's Loaded Weapon 1.* That same year Estrada, who grew up in New York's Spanish Harlem, won superstar status south of the border by appearing as a Latino Romeo in a Mexican soap, *Two Women, One Direction.* Later, back in the States, he joined the CBS soap *The Bold and the Beautiful* and did guest shots on prime time. A twice-divorced father of two sons, he married Nanette Mirkovich, a production coordinator he'd met at a gym, in 1997. Estrada has mellowed a bit since his Ponch days, but, noted Mirkovich, "he still has the best buns."

GEORGE CLOONEY

Born: May 6, 1961

RESIDENT HEARTTHROB As Doug Ross, the rakishly handsome pediatrician on NBC's *ER*, George Clooney set pulses racing playing a sexier, hipper version of the more paternal Drs. Kildare and Welby—a troubled bad boy with a heart of gold. "This was a character George had been waiting to play his whole life," said friend and former costar Julianna Margulies. Indeed, it was a long time coming. Starting in TV as a boy, handling cue cards on his father's Cincinnati talk show, Clooney landed his first steady onscreen job in his early 20s on a series titled, ironically, *E/R,* this one a mercifully short-lived CBS hospital comedy. He then toiled for 10 years as what he called "the world's richest unknown actor" in recurring roles on hit series—*The Facts of Life, Roseanne, Sisters*—and survived 15 failed pilots before becoming super-known with *ER* in 1994.

It earned him two Emmy nominations, and he never took the show for granted. "I don't think of *ER* as a stepping stone," he said early on. "This is what you fight to get into, not what you fight to get away from." But when his contract wound down in 1999, Clooney did leave to star in such envelope-pushing films as *Three Kings* and *Confessions of a Dangerous Mind* (also his directorial debut). He did return to the small screen in 2000 to produce a live remake of the 1964 nuclear-nightmare film *Fail-Safe* for CBS. A renowned bachelor (his three-year marriage to actress Talia Balsam ended in 1992), Clooney lives in L.A. with longtime companion Max, a 150-lb. potbellied pig. Despite his $20 million-a-film paycheck, he jokes that someday he'll be the center on *Hollywood Squares*. Not likely. "I've never seen anybody deal with fame better," said prescient *ER* castmate Noah Wyle in 1996. "Mark my words: He's going to be an enormous star."

PIERCE BROSNAN

Born: May 16, 1952

BONDED STEELE The world knows him today as "Bond, James Bond"—the fifth actor to take over the most famous action franchise in movie history. Ironically, Brosnan, who first uttered that signature line in 1995's *GoldenEye,* could have roared off in Bond's Aston Martin nine years earlier—had he been able to wriggle out of the title role of TV's *Remington Steele.* That was the suave, debonair con artist hired by Stephanie Zimbalist to front her L.A. private-detective agency. Much *Moonlighting*-style banter ensued between the feckless fraud and his uptight employer. But Brosnan, an Irish actor who had made his prime-time debut in the 1981 miniseries *The Manions of America,* was furious that his ironclad *Steele* contract locked him into one more season (his fifth) on the NBC series—and thus killed a dream deal to succeed Roger Moore as 007. It was small consolation at the time that Brosnan might never have been considered if it weren't for the *Steele* showcase. *Goldfinger,* he said, "was the first movie I ever saw," and he had long felt destined to fill the part. The role went to Timothy Dalton instead. After *Steele* ended, Brosnan soldiered on in films like *The Fourth Protocol* and *Mrs. Doubtfire* until the Bond producers reapproached him.

Now, with four 007 missions under his belt, Brosnan has shown that he's ready to move on to dramatically meatier fare. He won raves as a corrupt, dissolute British agent, the flip side of Bond, in *The Tailor of Panama,* and also impressed critics as an unemployed single father seeking to regain custody of his children in *Evelyn.* Brosnan himself has a son and two stepchildren by his first wife, actress Cassandra Harris (a former Bond girl in *For Your Eyes Only*), who died of ovarian cancer in 1991, and two more sons by TV reporter Keely Shaye Smith, whom he wed 10 years later. "His family and his wife come first," said his *Die Another Day* costar Halle Berry. "They were always on the set with him. He's a mensch in my book." For his part, Brosnan, who helped son Sean, then 16, recover from a near-fatal car accident in 2000, is philosophical. "I believe in fate," he said. "The bad things, you have to find the strength to go through it. And the good things you just enjoy."

Born: October 16, 1946

SUZANNE SOMERS

MAKEOVER QUEEN "I think in retrospect it's funny that Chrissy Snow was the first feminist on television," said Suzanne Somers of the giggly blonde bombshell she played on *Three's Company.* "I mean, here I am with the hot pants, the sassy ponytails and the knee-high socks asking for equality." Of course, it wasn't the sex-kittenish and clearly unfeminist Chrissy she was referring to but Somers herself, who was demanding financial parity with male stars of the '70s like *M*A*S*H*'s Alan Alda. She succeeded only in infuriating *Company*'s producers, who rejected her pay-hike request, and in alienating castmates John Ritter and Joyce DeWitt. The upshot: In 1981, after four seasons, Somers was replaced, and found her series career at a dead end. Undaunted, she bounced back as the supple TV spokeswoman for the ThighMaster and ButtMaster. She and manager husband Alan Hamel (with whom she raised her son, Bruce, from a previous marriage) now head a merchandising empire of fitness books, food and skin-care products. Her most heroic comeback has been battling breast cancer, for which she was treated in 2000 with surgery, radiation and—spurning chemo—her own regimen of hormone therapy. This year she launched a one-woman stage show called *Blonde in the Thunderbird*—a nostalgic nod to her splashy film debut three decades ago in *American Graffiti.*

DAVID HASSELHOFF

Born: July 17, 1952

MR. SAND MAN He could have been just another TV hunk in trunks. But as star as well as an executive producer of *Baywatch*, David Hasselhoff has shown he has brains as well as pecs. A onetime soap stud on *The Young and the Restless,* he leaped to prime-time stardom in the '80s in *Knight Rider,* as Michael Knight, a crime fighter partnered with KITT, a futuristic talking car. "Be careful, Michael," KITT would warn. For his next series Hasselhoff decided he would *really* be in the driver's seat. *Baywatch* was a one-season wonder on NBC in 1990 which Hasselhoff revived in syndication by enticing foreign investors. This time he not only starred as head lifeguard Mitch Buchannon but also took charge behind the scenes. Hasselhoff's entrepreneurial smarts (low production costs, lots of jiggle) helped turn the series into an international hit from Ireland to Outer Mongolia. Though wags quickly derided the show as *Buttwatch,* Hasselhoff determined to transcend its T&A formula in later seasons by emphasizing what he called "emotional" plotlines. "I love family-entertainment stuff that makes you cry," he said. "I'm from the Michael Landon school." He has cried all the way to the bank. The show has made a fortune worldwide; Hasselhoff's cut as part owner is 25 percent. In 1995, seeking to extend his Midas touch, he launched a spin-off, *Baywatch Nights,* which, like its predecessor, became a monster hit abroad. Hasselhoff can also thank his European fans for his success as a recording artist. (In Germany, his popularity has rivaled that of Madonna and Michael Jackson.) "I see myself doing the stuff that Michael Bolton does," he said, "or country pop." His voice carried him to Broadway in 2000 as the title star of *Jekyll & Hyde.* A *Baywatch* TV-movie reunion aired last winter, but the road to fame and riches has occasionally been bumpy. In 2002 Hasselhoff checked himself into the Betty Ford Center for a stint of alcohol rehab. Recently he and his second wife, Pamela Bach (a former *Baywatch* regular with whom he has two daughters), suffered fractures and other injuries after a motorcycle crash in Los Angeles. Both are now recovered. Still . . . be careful, David.

TOM SELLECK

Born: January 29, 1945

ALOHA, ADONIS In *Magnum, P.I.,* Tom Selleck lived the ultimate male fantasy. As macho mustachioed private investigator Thomas Magnum, Selleck tooled around in a snazzy red Ferrari and lounged about in shorts, rent-free, on a lush Hawaiian estate, Robin's Nest, owned (as was the car) by Magnum's absentee employer, Robin Masters. Not a bad life for a gumshoe—or for a onetime contestant on *The Dating Game* in the '60s who worked his way up from a stud on *The Young and the Restless* to a zombified hospital patient in the 1978 film *Coma.* Two years later, his *Magnum* exposure changed everything. The lanky 6'4" star had become so popular that he was tapped to star in the blockbuster-to-be *Raiders of the Lost Ark.* Unfortunately, CBS held him to his series contract, so the role of Indiana Jones went instead to a then up-and-coming Harrison Ford. Selleck did get to moonlight in other action flicks, such as *High Road to China, Lassiter* and *Runaway.* But his biggest hit proved to be a comedy, 1987's *Three Men and a Baby.* Later films were not so successful. "Some people say I should have quit *Magnum* a year earlier, right after *Three Men,*" he said. "But there are a lot of second and third acts in this business." He should know. Since the '90s Selleck has beefed up his résumé back in TV, first in a recurring role as Courteney Cox's much older lover on *Friends* and then in a series of burly made-for-cable Westerns. He and second wife Jillie Mack are also home on the range—raising daughter Hannah on their 21-acre organic-avocado ranch north of L.A. Though not as exotic as Robin's Nest, it satisfies Selleck. "Twenty years after *Magnum,*" he said, "I'm grateful that people still want me."

HEATHER LOCKLEAR

Born: September 25, 1961

SURVIVOR: HOLLYWOOD "Better to have longevity than be a flash in the pan," said Heather Locklear. A California-born, sunshine-and-spitfire actress whose career spans two decades, Locklear knows whereof she speaks. In the '80s alone she doubled our pleasure—vamping it up as conniving vixen Sammy Jo Dean on *Dynasty* while simultaneously costarring as plucky rookie cop Stacy Sheridan on *T.J. Hooker.* In the '90s (and in her 30s), Locklear graduated to a seductive older woman, Amanda Woodward, the manipulative landlady of *Melrose Place,* a show about a Gen-X swinging-singles L.A. apartment complex. And then, for a surprising comic turn, she joined *Spin City* in 1999 as hard-driving mayoral campaign manager Caitlin Moore. Now that's longevity. Ironically, Locklear, the youngest of four children (her dad was a UCLA administrator, her mom a Disney production exec), had been so shy in high school that she took an F rather than deliver a monologue in drama class. Still, she was game and determined enough to drop out of UCLA her freshman year to do TV commercials before landing on *Dynasty* at 19. "You'd think Heather was so sweet and innocent that she should star in *Little Women,*" said Aaron Spelling, executive producer of both *Dynasty* and *T.J. Hooker.* "But she has a streak that likes fast cars and tattoos [she has three, including "a rose and a heart mushed together" on her ankle, she revealed] and rock stars." In fact, joked Locklear, "I don't date rock and rollers; I just marry them." First there was Mötley Crüe drummer Tommy Lee, whom she divorced after seven stormy years. In 1994 she wed Bon Jovi lead guitarist Richie Sambora, with whom she has a daughter, Ava. "One of the best things is just how close it's made Richie and me," she said of Ava's arrival, "because now we think, 'Look what we did! It's absolutely amazing.' "

QUICK STUDY Bruce Willis was a Manhattan bartender, prematurely balding and with minimal acting experience, when he beat out 3,000 competitors to play Cybill Shepherd's cocky antagonist in 1985's titanic hit *Moonlighting*. "The show was my Ph.D.," said Willis, a New Jersey-bred college dropout. He graduated from TV four seasons later with Emmy honors, having already established himself in films in the 1987 romantic comedy *Blind Date*. That same year he met and married Demi Moore. Between headlining in blockbusters (including his *Die Hard* series), the couple escaped to the seclusion of Hailey, Idaho, where they raised their three daughters—Rumer, Scout and Tallulah. But conflicting shooting schedules contributed to the surprise demise of their decade-long marriage—if not their friendship. "I'm so glad to still have Demi in my life. We probably get along better now," said Willis, who still celebrates holidays with the girls, Moore and sometimes his or her significant other. Papa Bruce returns at least monthly to Hailey, where he owns a manse across from Moore's. Now a party-monger emeritus, Willis declared, "All I've learned is that I want to live my life as a good man and a good father."

BRUCE WILLIS

Born: March 19, 1955

LONI ANDERSON

Born: August 5, 1945

HEAD TURNER With its hip deejays Venus Flytrap and Dr. Johnny Fever and addled newsman Les Nessman, the 1978-82 sitcom *WKRP in Cincinnati* was a frenetic fun house of eccentrics and misfits—except, it seemed, when Jennifer Marlowe, the radio station's receptionist, made her entrance. Then it was all viewers could do to peel their eyes off Loni Anderson's cashmere-bound figure. Of course, it was her luscious lips that delivered the show's sharpest barbs. And why not? Anderson had been a Minnesota high school teacher before she got hooked by community theater. Still, as she noted, "it wasn't until I became a blonde that my career started moving." The former brunette proved to be a deft comic actress on *WKRP* and, backstage, had a flaming affair with Gary Sandy, who played hunky program director Andy Travis. It had ended before Burt Reynolds coaxed her into a 1981 New Year's weekend at his Florida ranch. He became her third husband in 1988. Four months later, Reynolds and Anderson (who has a daughter, Deidra, from her first marriage) adopted an infant son, Quinton. In 1993 the couple went through a screaming divorce. "Burt had a [prescription] drug problem and a bad temper," she claimed. Since then, Anderson has lived with corporate attorney Geoff Brown. She went on to do three more series (including *Partners in Crime* with Lynda Carter) and guest shots (such as Pamela Anderson's sexy mama on *V.I.P.*). How does she continue to look so fine in her 50s? Anderson has admitted to having twice had breast *reduction* surgery, among other cosmetic refinements. "Since I want to be a working actress until they carry me away," she stated, "I've always said that I intend to live long enough to have everything lifted."

ANTHONY GEARY

Born: May 29, 1947

COOL HAND LUKE The 1981 nuptials of Luke Spencer and Laura Baldwin on *General Hospital* drew an estimated 30 million viewers—and still ranks as one of the highest-rated moments in soap history. Yet for Anthony Geary, who played the ne'er-do-well groom, fame had its downside. He was horrified, he said, when female fans cried out, "Rape me, Luke!"—a reference to the controversial scene that ignited the Luke and Laura romance. And the fans were everywhere. "There was a time when I wasn't able to leave my house," said the Utah-born L.A. resident. He finally left *GH* in 1984, three years after Genie Francis (Laura) quit. Geary's wan, frizzy-haired charisma didn't quite take hold in prime time, where he was cast in TV flicks like *Intimate Agony* as a doctor battling a herpes epidemic. After a run of unmemorable films (*High Desert Kill, Penitentiary III*), he was enticed back to *GH* in 1991—but only on the condition that he not have to reprise his old character. "Basically, I didn't want to do Luke without Laura," he said. Instead, he played Luke's look-alike cousin Bill until Francis's return two years later restoked the L&L show. They divorced in 2001, but Geary, a confirmed bachelor himself, vowed to hang in as Luke. "As I get older," he conceded, "I realize having this role is a pretty damn good gig."

TOUGH CUSTOMERS

WHETHER THEY WORK A BEAT OR MANIPULATE A DYNASTY, GO UNDERCOVER OR ABOVE THE LAW, THESE AGENTS, OFFICERS, WISEGUYS AND DRAMA QUEENS GAVE US A JOLT WITH GRIT, WIT AND FIREPOWER

JENNIFER GARNER

Born: April 17, 1972

KICK CHICK When a family pet triggered the burglar alarm one night last year at the L.A. home of Jennifer Garner and actor husband Scott Foley (*Felicity*), the couple (who have since separated) crept downstairs looking for an intruder. Foley had a baseball bat, and Garner was behind him, thinking, Elbow? Knee to the crotch? Backspin hook kick? With her brunette locks and full-lipped smile, Garner looks like the coed next door, but violence has now become second nature. As double agent (and troubled grad student) Sydney Bristow of ABC's *Alias,* the former ballet student has chopped and socked and gouged her way to a Best Actress Golden Globe (over Edie Falco) and won the attention of fans like Quentin Tarantino, who did a villainous cameo last season. "You're gonna work forever," he told her. "You don't have to prove nothin' to nobody." Except to herself, of course. "I wasn't naturally talented," the West Virginian has said, "just really, really driven." Between TV shootings, Garner costarred on the big screen as Elektra, Ben Affleck's avenging ninja girlfriend in the Marvel Comics-inspired hit *Daredevil.* Her moves were so impressive that an Elektra spinoff is under consideration, which gives Garner a new kick. "Sydney fights because she has to," she said. "Elektra is out for blood."

JAMES GANDOLFINI

Born: September 18, 1961

THE BOSS Thanks to *The Sopranos,* James Gandolfini has been a made man since the HBO series' launch in 1999. What has been unsettling is the bada-bing effect on female fans. "That sex-symbol thing is so freaky to me," Gandolfini marveled. "I'm the guy on TV in that lovely terry cloth robe with his big gut hanging out. I mean, come on. It's weird." Not so, says his costar in 2001's *The Mexican,* Julia Roberts. "There's something so amazing with what James does with Tony Soprano," she said. "I mean, here he is, a cold-blooded killer, and we love him! We feel bad for him." Gandolfini, who has a young son with ex-wife Marcy, is currently dating director's assistant Lora Somoza. Despite film credits like *True Romance* and *Get Shorty* and his two Emmys for *The Sopranos*, the New York City actor still frets about his future. "I don't feel that anything's been proven yet in terms of my career," he has said. "I'm playing an Italian lunatic from New Jersey, and that's basically what I am." *Capisce?*

DON JOHNSON

Born: December 15, 1949

LOTHARIO LAWMAN Showbiz, like the divine, works in mysterious ways. In 1983, struggling actor Don Johnson had made a few so-so films, been to alcoholism rehab and was known at NBC as a "six-time loser" (six failed pilots). A year later, he was one of TV's hottest heartthrobs. As fast-living (and loving) detective Sonny Crockett of *Miami Vice* (1984-89), he added a flirty wink to the predictable scripts and made stubble a cheeky sex symbol. With its MTV-like style, *Vice* was a small-screen phenomenon, and Johnson's duds—white sport jacket over a pastel T-shirt—became a singles-bar uniform. The Missouri native lived the image offscreen, too. Nicknamed Don Juanson, he has had a stream of ladies, from his U. of Kansas drama teacher to Barbra Streisand, who recorded a duet with him of "Till I Loved You." Johnson racked up four failed marriages, two of them to Melanie Griffith. When their second five-year hitch famously tanked, he hit the bottle again. "Some people fall off the wagon," he said. "I fell off a building." But he wasn't down for long. The dad of four wed socialite Kelley Phleger in 1999, and starred in another hit series, *Nash Bridges.* "He's taken his lumps," said *Bridges* costar Cheech Marin. "But he'll still be standing in the 15th round."

Born: December 23, 1946

SUSAN LUCCI

SOAP SIREN Susan Lucci thought it was typecasting when she was picked to play spoiled teen Erica Kane on ABC's fledgling soap *All My Children.* "I was a self-centered, haughty girl," she said. But no one, especially the diminutive Long Island native, foresaw that, 33 years later, she would still be camping it up as man-eating Erica, daytime's most famous character by several hair extensions. Erica has run through nine marriages, impersonated a nun and gone to Betty Ford, all without chipping a nail. Despite her renown, Lucci was nominated—and rejected—18 times for a Lead Actress Emmy before she finally scored in 1999. The losing streak became a pop-culture joke, but, as pal Joan Rivers pointed out, "everyone knows who she is because of it." A mom of two and wife for 34 years of her manager, Helmut Huber, Lucci anguishes over her near-nightly burden of 50 pages of script. "In my next life I'd like to come back as a homebody or an actress," she said. "There's not enough time to be both."

Born: May 21, 1952

MR. T

CELEBRITY COMMANDO "Betta watch out, sucka!" So warned Mr. T as B.A. (Bad Attitude) Baracus on almost every episode of NBC's mid-'80s smash *The A-Team.* He meant it. Sporting an in-your-face Mohawk and 35 lbs. of gold chains (symbolic, he said, of slavery), Mr. T was one of a superhero squad fighting for right with cartoonish violence. *Team* made him a star; his mouth made him a celebrity. He noted of his character, "He's big, he's bad, and he's black." Born Lawrence Tureaud in a Chicago ghetto, he took on the Mr. T appellation and persona to market himself as a bodyguard, and wound up with clients like Michael Jackson and Steve McQueen. His startling look led to a featured role in 1982's *Rocky III.* But after *A-Team,* his life turned B-list for a while. The father of three made TV appearances and a movie or two but was mostly unemployed by the mid-'90s. Worse, he was successfully sued for $4.9 million by two Chicago men who claimed they helped him create the Mr. T persona. In 1995, he contracted T-cell lymphoma, a rare cancer recently in remission. "I got my swagger back," he said, and resurrected his pop iconhood as a pitchman for the phone service 1-800-COLLECT. But illness has mellowed him. Chemo wiped out his Mohawk, and he gave his jewelry to family members. "I don't wear gold no more," said Mr. T. "The gold is in my heart."

DAVID CARUSO

Born: January 7, 1956

GOOD COP, BAD COP Playing John Kelly, *NYPD Blue*'s hard-bitten detective, David Caruso was often upstaged by his own bare butt. But executive producer Steven Bochco, who had earlier tapped the Queens-born actor to play an Irish gang leader on *Hill Street Blues,* saw a more dimensional potential. "He's a working-class guy, and I like offbeat characters," he said. "He's just a terrific package." The über-intense Caruso patterned himself after another carrot-topped New Yorker, Jimmy Cagney, as he ping-ponged between TV and film roles until 1993, when he landed the character close to his heart. "For John Kelly to care about people and not be burned out by the poison he's absorbing in his job," he said, "well, that makes him the ultimate stand-up guy I aspire to be." He would have a way to go. Along with an Emmy nod, Caruso earned a rep for being temperamental—which he jokingly acknowledged by taping a "Mr. Difficult" sign to his chair. But just four episodes into the second season, he defected to pursue a film career. After flops like *Jade* and *Kiss of Death* he returned to series TV with the one-season legal drama *Michael Hayes,* but it wasn't until 2002, as forensic investigator Horatio Caine on CBS's *CSI: Miami,* that the viewers really welcomed him back. "Caruso," wrote *The Washington Post*'s Tom Shales, "has lost none of [his] magnetism." With steady work, homes in Miami and L.A. and a third wife, Margaret Buckley, and a daughter, Greta (from a second marriage), Caruso is at peace with his past. "In a way," he said, "my life began after all of that went away—the shift from needing acting to substantiate my identity to thinking of myself as a working actor who has a wonderful marriage, a great daughter and a good life."

QUEEN OF MEAN "You have to be a very nice woman to play a bitch," Joan Collins told Oprah. "Or it doesn't work." Bad news, Joan dahling. Much as you'd like to soften your image, we'll always see you as Alexis Carrington Colby, that high-living, catfighting vixen you played for eight seasons on *Dynasty.* The scenes are indelible: Alexis, clad in Nolan Miller power shoulders, duking it out with rival Krystle Carrington (Linda Evans) in a mud puddle; or that over-the-balcony tumble with ex-hubby Dex. For the London-born actress dubbed "the poor man's Elizabeth Taylor," *Dynasty* paid off with a Golden Globe and new respect. "There's almost a regal air about her," noted *Pacific Palisades* costar Brittney Powell. Off-set, she was definitely Windsor-esque. As Collins has said, "There was more drama going on in my personal life than in front of the camera." She dated Warren Beatty and Ryan O'Neal, and was divorced four times before marrying theatrical manager Percy Gibson in 2002. Today, between roles, the resilient mother of three and grandma of one has become, like younger sister Jackie, a bestselling novelist. "A career is like a seesaw," she joked of her 40-plus years in showbiz. "I've gone from babe to bitch to bag."

JOAN COLLINS

Born: May 23, 1933

KIEFER SUTHERLAND

Born: December 21, 1966

ALL-DAY AGENT For two seasons now, Kiefer Sutherland has been having a very bad day every week. As agent Jack Bauer on FOX's Emmy-nominated hit *24,* he has had to foil an assassination, find his missing daughter, bury his wife and expose a mole in the agency. Playing the soulful, angst-ridden Bauer on the series, which takes place in real time over the course of a day (24 hours equals 24 episodes), won the Toronto-raised Sutherland a Golden Globe and a female following including costar Leslie Hope, who says he has "the patience of a saint, is a good listener—and his butt looks awesome in his Wranglers!" All butts aside, it was not always so. The son of actors Donald Sutherland and Shirley Douglas liked to party hearty with *Young Guns* pals and was spotted with a go-go dancer just weeks before his planned 1991 wedding to Julia Roberts, who famously left him at the altar. After two failed marriages, a mellower Sutherland, whose films run from *Stand by Me* to this year's *Phone Booth,* finds more time now to hang and play with daughter Sarah Jude (by actress Camelia Kath). "I'm lucky," he says. "Life is kind of moving on."

Born: October 28, 1944

DENNIS FRANZ

TOP COP Balding, jowly and great of girth, Dennis Franz has played 28 different cops in his career, none more memorably or longer (10 seasons) than *NYPD Blue*'s Andy Sipowicz. In lesser hands the hardened detective—racist, misogynistic, alcoholic and terminally cranky—would seem beyond redemption. "This is the lowest I've ever been able to play a character," said the Chicago native and Vietnam vet. Basically, Franz transformed Sipowicz into a sympathetic mass of contradictions and the emotional heart of the show (and an unlikely sex symbol after a 1994 episode featuring his bare behind produced a ratings spike). "The dimension and subtlety and depth Dennis brings to that character are something to see," said *Blue* co-creator David Milch. Industry peers concurred, awarding him four Emmys. In 1995 the antique-loving flea-market regular married his lady of 18 years, corporate promotions exec Joanie Zeck, whose two daughters he had dotingly helped raise (and who took his name after the wedding). "There comes a time when metabolism, numerical age and enthusiasm all mesh," he said. "For me, it didn't happen when I was 20. It's happening now."

MARG HELGENBERGER

Born: November 16, 1958

HARDBOILED SWEETHEART From a heroin-addicted hooker to a tireless forensic investigator, Marg Helgenberger found her characters mostly falling on one side of the law or the other. Not that she's complaining. "I either play cops or criminals," she said. "I gravitate toward edgier material because it suits my nature." The Nebraska native got her start in 1982 as a spunky rookie cop on the ABC soap *Ryan's Hope*. Six years later she lit up prime time with her Emmy-winning portrayal of prostitute K.C. Koloski on ABC's Vietnam drama *China Beach*. "Marg could loll in a doorway like Lauren Bacall and the great actresses of the '40s," said John Sacret Young, the series creator. "She was so cool—yet there were always fires burning inside." After *Beach* was canceled in 1991, Helgenberger kept those fires stoked in projects on film (she played the cancer victim whose case spurred the lawsuit in *Erin Brockovich*) and TV (she had a recurring role as the love interest of George Clooney's Doug Ross on *ER*). But roles weren't always easy to come by. "The comment I get most often is 'Too old and too pretty,'" she said at the time. "And I'm thinking, So if I were younger and uglier I'd have more of a career?" In 2000, the sultry redhead was welcomed back to the weekly grind on CBS's *CSI: Crime Scene Investigation*. As stripper turned criminologist Catherine Willows, Helgenberger is "hands down a pro," said costar Gary Dourdan. "I call her Margalicious. She brings a real sexuality to her role, a bit of a rough edge." But for all her tough-chick bravado, the gritty world of *CSI* has proved a challenge. "I'm relatively squeamish in civilian life," she said. "When we're filming autopsy scenes, I actually feel sad." Offscreen she's more likely to feel happy, now that the series has allowed her to nest in Santa Monica with her husband of 14 years, actor Alan Rosenberg, and son Hugh. Is there anything that could tempt her to fly the coop for a while? Sure, she said. "If Steven Spielberg or Steven Soderbergh or any number of directors were to say, 'Hey, there's this role, are you interested?' I'd be there in a flash."

SIGNIFICANT OTHERS

JUST AS THE MOON SOMETIMES ECLIPSES THE SUN, A FEW LESS CELESTIAL BEINGS LIKE KRAMER, URKEL, J.J. AND MIMI TWINKLED TO UNLIKELY STARDOM; SEVERAL EVEN GOT THEIR OWN SHOW—BRIEFLY

MICHAEL RICHARDS

As Seinfeld's nutty, hot-wired neighbor, Cosmo Kramer slid, skidded and stumbled his way through the door each week and into the comedy galaxy. Like his bizarre get-rich-quick schemes, his follow-up, *The Michael Richards Show,* bombed. Without the crowd-pleasing Kramer quirks, he got the hook after six weeks.

KATHY KINNEY

Her gruff attitude, cartoonish wardrobe and five shades of blue eye shadow helped Kinney parlay a onetime guest shot as Mimi "the coworker from hell" into a scene-stealing regular gig on *The Drew Carey Show*.

SEAN HAYES
MEGAN MULLALLY

Some episodes of *Will & Grace* might be retitled *Jack & Karen*. Hayes played the wisecracking, more flamboyant best friend of the gay lead, and Mullally was the heroine's spoiled socialite secretary.

TED KNIGHT

Amid a veritable all-star ensemble on *The Mary Tyler Moore Show,* the vain and vacuous anchor Ted Baxter won two Emmys and even landed a cameo from a better-trusted TV newscaster, Walter Cronkite (right).

ROBERT PASTORELLI

She didn't know why Eldin popped up in her house at all hours, but Murphy Brown appreciated the ready ear of her eccentric housepainter and eventual nanny. His own starring series, *Double Rush,* turned out a four-month dud.

CHRISTOPHER LLOYD

Taxi's spaced-out "Reverend Jim" Ignatowski (with Judd Hirsch, right) wound up with more worshipful fans than flock—and two Emmys.

JALEEL WHITE

The nasally whine, oversize specs and high-water pants helped *Family Matters'* über-nerd Steve Urkel turn a guest spot in 1989 into a focal role for the show's seven-year run.

RON PALILLO

A laugh reminiscent of a squawking bird helped Horshack (center, with Gabe Kaplan, left, John Travolta and classmates) become one of the most annoyingly endearing sweathogs in *Welcome Back, Kotter.*

RICHARD MOLL

As the towering, bald and sometimes bare bailiff on *Night Court,* "Bull" Shannon remained the courtroom comedy's bulwark for the eight years until its '92 adjournment.

POLLY HOLLIDAY

"Kiss mah grits" was her signature riposte as the saucy, Texas-twanged waitress on *Alice.* CBS was encouraged enough to headline her in a spin-off, *Flo,* but it fizzled out in its first season.

JACKEE HARRY

As the resident vamp of the apartment house in *227*, Sandra shook her booty in tight dresses, flirted with every man in sight and was the lightning to star Marla Gibbs, a thunder-stealer earlier herself (see page 117).

MICHAEL McKEAN & DAVID L. LANDER

In the 1950s-set comedy *Laverne & Shirley*, McKean (left) and Lander played Lenny and Squiggy, girl-crazy truck drivers at the Shotz Brewery. The show was also famous for the backstage tension between stars Penny Marshall and Cindy Williams.

HERVE VILLECHAIZE

As Ricardo Montalban's reliable sidekick on *Fantasy Island,* the 3'11" Tattoo delivered one of TV's most over-quoted lines: "De plane, de plane!"

JIMMIE WALKER

An equally famous catchphrase, "Dy-no-mité," came from *Good Times'* irresistible J.J. The star, Esther Rolle, left the show for two years in protest of what she felt was his buffoonish, racially demeaning character.

PAT HARRINGTON

As the building super and self-proclaimed Lothario on *One Day at a Time,* Schneider became an unlikely father figure to the headstrong teen girls played by Valerie Bertinelli and Mackenzie Phillips. As ubiquitous as Schneider was through the nine years, no one ever used his first name, which was Dwayne.

WILLIAM SANDERSON, TONY PAPENFUSS & JOHN VOLDSTAD

These scraggly, scene-stealing siblings on *Newhart* didn't have a last name. Two of the brothers never uttered a word in eight years on the air, so Sanderson (left) handled the weekly introduction. "I'm Larry," he said. "This is my brother Darryl. And this is my other brother Darryl."

MARLA GIBBS

She was booked to appear on just one 1975 episode of *The Jeffersons,* but her character, Florence the maid (with Isabel Sanford, right), proved essential as a sharp-tongued counterforce to her petulant boss George. When the show wound down in '85, she moved on up to her own successful sitcom, *227.*

DR. MIKE QUINN, SPECIAL AGENT DALE COOPER, D.A. JACK McCOY . . . FROM CABOT COVE TO *THE WEST WING,* THESE SOLID CITIZENS BECAME THE PRIDE OF PRIME TIME—AND MADE US ALL FEEL A LITTLE SAFER IN THE MORNING

CROWD PLEASERS

JANE SEYMOUR

Born: February 15, 1951

HEART DOCTOR En route to becoming uncrowned queen of the miniseries, Jane Seymour played the Duchess of Windsor, Hemingway's Lady Brett Ashley and Maria Callas. For that last role, as the diva of divas, she won an Emmy. But it wasn't until the British-born actress traded her Continental finery for cotton petticoats in *Dr. Quinn, Medicine Woman,* that she emerged as a U.S. fixture. From its debut on New Year's Day, 1993, the feminist Western about a young woman doctor who settles in the wilds of Colorado was an unexpected popular success. "I don't think the critics even really watched it," Seymour said. "I think they just kind of put it on and went, 'Oh, it's soft, it's not *Northern Exposure,* it's not quirky, it looks normal,' and therefore passed." The frontier saga gave CBS its first Saturday-night hit since *The Mary Tyler Moore Show* in 1977 and netted Seymour a Golden Globe. Growing up outside London, Joyce Frankenberg (as she was born) was a physician's daughter and aspiring ballerina who switched to acting when her knees gave out at 16. She gained fame (or notoriety) six years later as the clairvoyant Bond girl Solitaire in *Live and Let Die.* Seymour has twin boys with her fourth husband, actor James Keach, two stepchildren and two children from an earlier marriage. Now Malibu-based (though she has a 15th-century manor house in England), she also writes books, paints and runs a clothing line. "She's a hard worker," said Mieke Frankenberg of her driven daughter. "And hard on herself."

STRAIGHT ARROW With a chin—and a moral compass—worthy of Dudley Do-Right, Special Agent Dale Cooper, who had a weakness for cherry pie and "a damn fine cup of coffee," was what passed for normal in the twilight zone of ABC's *Twin Peaks.* Director David Lynch, who created the early-'90s cult series, chose Kyle MacLachlan to play Cooper because "he's the person you trust enough to go into a strange world with." They had worked together on the films *Dune* and *Blue Velvet,* and *Peaks* picked up 17 Emmy nominations, including two for MacLachlan. But the show's increasingly bizarro plot line soon frustrated the actor. "It became weird for weird's sake," he said. The plug was pulled after two seasons. For the rest of the '90s the Yakima, Washington, native made lackluster TV movies and big-screen bombs like *Showgirls.* In 2000 his clean-cut TV pedigree landed him on HBO's *Sex and the City* as Charlotte's straitlaced—and impotent—doctor husband. Executive producer Michael Patrick King noted that the "flat, flaccid preppy" was the antithesis of MacLachlan, who had high-octane romances with Lara Flynn Boyle and Laura Dern, and was once engaged to model Linda Evangelista. These days, though, he shares bicoastal homes with his publicist wife Desiree Gruber, and this summer he added a small film, *Northfork,* to his dossier. "I've taken some heavy hits," he admitted. "But the fact that I'm still here feels good."

KYLE MACLACHLAN

Born: February 22, 1959

SAM WATERSTON

Born: November 15, 1940

THE REAL McCOY Perps committing crimes on *Law & Order* had to contend not only with Sam Waterston's canny calm and deliberate strength—but also with his supernaturally expressive eyebrows. As crusading Manhattan district attorney Jack McCoy, he raised them skyward while railing for justice and snapped them down to glower at transgressors during courtroom battles that were, bragged the show's promos, "ripped from today's headlines." The series became NBC's longest-running current drama (13 seasons and counting) because—just like in the news stories—he sometimes lost. "We don't wrap up the moral questions in a comfortable way," explained Waterston. Indeed, his McCoy had a fondness for both motorcycles and the bottle, and used his facts judiciously to make his case. "The bad guys don't always get punished," he said, "and the good guys are not necessarily pure."

Lean and patrician ("In another 20 years he could pose for Uncle Sam posters," noted one reviewer), the Massachusetts-bred, Yale-grad son of an academic and an artist has made a career of playing tormented men in ethically tight spots. He was the conflicted father of the atom bomb in the PBS miniseries *Oppenheimer* before playing Abe Lincoln twice—on Broadway and in the TV movie *Gore Vidal's Lincoln.* Before and after his Oscar-nominated turn as a conscience-stricken war correspondent in 1984's *The Killing Fields* came parts in four Woody Allen movies and two seasons spent as a prosecuting attorney coming to grips with an integrating South in the acclaimed drama *I'll Fly Away.* Directing him was "like driving a Rolls-Royce," said that show's executive producer, and Waterston counts on adding a few more miles, although he has settled with wife Lynn in rural Connecticut. (They have three children, and he has a son from an earlier marriage.) "I like moving between all three media—theater, movies, TV," he once explained. "But for telling an ongoing story, there's nothing like television."

SELA WARD

Born: July 11, 1956

LATE BLOOMER Drew Barrymore debuted at 3. Julia Roberts was rolling by 19. As for Sela Ward, she was making a career in advertising, modeling on the side, and only at 27, after becoming Maybelline's new face, did she decide to move to L.A. and study acting. Then it took another eight years before her breakthrough on NBC's soapy, heartrending *Sisters*. Playing the alcoholic black-sheep sister Teddy Reed was a stretch. "I was a good girl, more Melanie Wilkes than Scarlett O'Hara," said Ward of her Mississippi childhood and cheerleading days at the University of Alabama. She stayed on *Sisters* all five years and won an Emmy but had had it with TV shooting schedules. By then she had married venture capitalist Howard Sherman and started a family (Austin and Anabella). She caught small film parts in *The Fugitive* and *Runaway Bride* but got the ultimate, perhaps inevitable Hollywood rejection when she auditioned to play a Bond girl. "At 40, I'd never felt as confident or attractive," recalled Ward. "Instead I was told, 'Too bad, you're too old. We want the Sela Ward of 10 years ago.' "

Ward got mad—and even—returning to television to produce a Lifetime documentary on ageism and to play divorced, lusty midlife mom Lily Manning on ABC's *Once and Again*. That was a welcome showcase for her lighter side, and she also appreciated the opportunities of the wardrobe. "Every time I get a script," she recalled, "it calls for me to be standing around in a bra and jeans." Billy Campbell, who shared her steamy scenes for three seasons as a divorced dad, said, "You'd have to be a fence post not to have chemistry with her." Also moved was the TV Academy, which voted Ward her second Emmy. "I've never felt yummier," she exulted in a recent interview. "I feel ripe and juicy, like a piece of fruit that's delicious."

CEREBRAL SLEUTH He cornered criminals and quoted Shakespeare. Solved mysteries and sautéed gourmet meals. As the star of *Spenser: For Hire,* Robert Urich revealed a classy melange of culture and real-life resolve to tackle it all. "I felt like this guy who could do anything you asked," Urich once proclaimed. He made good that boast on his résumé, which includes regular roles on some 15 series—a record probably unrivaled in the annals of television. But the tough, no-nonsense persona seen on *S.W.A.T., Vega$* and *Spenser* proved to be Urich's trademark—even if it was only an act. "His macho looks are deceptive," said wife Heather Menzies, who portrayed Louisa in *The Sound of Music* movie and with whom Urich adopted three children. "He's a very sensitive man." Yet nonetheless tenacious. In 1996, Urich, the self-described "uptight Catholic boy" from Ohio, was diagnosed with synovial sarcoma—a rare cancer of the joints that he fought for six years. But he still doggedly pursued work. "I thought, 'Let me exhibit the courage I've always seemed to display,'" asserted Urich, who toured with the musical *Chicago* and starred in 2001's *Emeril* before his death at 55. Of his final moments, Menzies recalled, "I held him and said, 'I want you to let go and come into my heart because it's safe there.' Now he's in my heart." And in ours.

ROBERT URICH

Born: December 19, 1946 Died: April 16, 2002

JIMMY SMITS

Born: July 9, 1955

TRAVELIN' MAN Hailed as a Latino heartthrob, Brooklyn-reared Jimmy Smits in fact boasts a more exotic heritage. "My mother is from Puerto Rico, and my father is from Suriname, a former Dutch colony in South America. His father was from Holland," said Smits, who lived briefly in Puerto Rico before his parents divorced. However varied his roots, the trim 6'3" actor proved universally irresistible when he joined *L.A. Law* in 1986 as fiercely idealistic attorney Victor Sifuentes. He departed five years later. "My contract was over and I just wanted to move on," said the 1990 Emmy winner. "It was never about leaving *L.A. Law* and becoming a giant movie star." Actually what was to have been his big breakout film—*Old Gringo,* in which he played a Mexican general opposite Gregory Peck and Jane Fonda—had already bombed at the box office in 1989. Smits went on to star in TV movies like *The Cisco Kid* and *Solomon & Sheba* (with a then-unknown Halle Berry).

He returned to glory in his next series, *NYPD Blue,* as soulful widowed detective Bobby Simone—filling the void left by the volatile David Caruso, who had quit during the show's second season to pursue his own movie career. Smits steamed up the screen in nude scenes with Kim Delaney as his precinct-house love interest and later wife. His quiet, laid-back intensity served as an effective foil to his hard-boiled beat partner (Dennis Franz). Then his four-year itch struck again. Bobby was killed off by an incurable heart infection in 1998 in perhaps the most drawn-out death since *Camille.* Smits, who has been involved with actress Wanda De Jesus for 18 years and has a son and daughter by ex-wife Barbara, whom he divorced in 1987, has subsequently nabbed starring roles in small films (the boxing drama *Price of Glory*) and small roles in blockbusters (including a scene as a senator in *Star Wars: Episode II—Attack of the Clones*). He even brushed up on his Shakespeare for a 2002 Off-Broadway revival of *Twelfth Night.* "Being versatile is what's beautiful about this business," he said. "You can be a cop, a lawyer, a king or a pauper."

Born: July 13, 1940

PATRICK STEWART

MR. UNIVERSE He boldly went where no Shakespearean actor had gone before: to the helm of a 24th-century spaceship, clad in red polyester. Hired in '87 for *Star Trek: The Next Generation*, Patrick Stewart was queasy about following in the footsteps of William Shatner, star of the original 1960s series. "For the first six weeks I was so scared I'd be fired that I didn't unpack a single bag in my hotel room," said the Yorkshire native. In fact he brought new gravitas to the captaincy, and his revival ran seven years. It also inspired four films, which Stewart starred in, and three spin-offs. Made an officer of the Order of the British Empire in 2001, he lives with producer wife Wendy Neuss in L.A., but they keep a home in England. (He has a grown son and daughter from his first marriage.) Today he is part of another powerful sci-fi franchise, as wheelchair-bound professor Charles Xavier in the *X-Men* films. But it's Jean-Luc Picard, and his trademark "Make it so," that made him an icon. Stewart plays along, admitting that "being in the captain's chair of the *Enterprise* is rather like sitting on the throne of England." Still, that's not to say he wouldn't like to see Trekkies expand their own horizons. "Wouldn't it be great," he once wondered, "if 4,000 people showed up at a Shakespeare convention?"

ANGELA LANSBURY

Born: October 16, 1925

MYSTERY WOMAN For 12 years, watching the bodies pile up in sleepy Cabot Cove, Maine, on CBS's *Murder, She Wrote* was a national pastime. Ranked among the Top 10 shows nearly every season, *Murder* spotlighted the talents of teacher-turned-mystery-writer Jessica Fletcher as she outfoxed dim-witted flatfoots and foiled hapless villains. The formula's appeal was no mystery to series star Angela Lansbury. "The show fulfills the natural human desire to solve a puzzle," she said. It also had the unsinkable (and un-P.C.) Jessica. "She's a man's woman," said Lansbury. "I think I am too. I think it has to do with being a professional woman, being very sure of oneself, having made one's mark." The London-born actress made hers in musical theater and films, accumulating four Tony Awards and three Oscar nominations for Best Supporting Actress before becoming America's favorite literary Sherlock in 1984. "I've never played a person who was close to myself until Jessica," she said. Even her husband of 53 years, Peter Shaw, who died of congestive heart failure in 2003 at age 84, said at the time that it was "awfully hard to tell the difference between the two. Angela has that marvelous gumption, and that's one of the nice things that Jessica has." But initially, the thought of revealing herself "frightened her," said former *Murder* executive producer Peter S. Fischer. "She was used to burying Angela Lansbury in a character. If you say to an audience, 'Hey, this is me!' and the audience doesn't like you, well, that would be crushing." She needn't have worried: She earned 12 Emmy nominations (but no trophies). Since the show ended in 1996, the Los Angeles resident and grandmother of three has done a number of *Murder* TV movies and provided voices for the animated features *Anastasia* and *Beauty and the Beast: The Enchanted Christmas.* But Jessica Fletcher lives on in her memory. "My dearest wish," she once wrote, "is that those who enjoyed Jessica's adventures will remember her as I do: an active, mature woman possessed of courage, independence and wit."

Born: August 3, 1940

MARTIN SHEEN

REFORM CANDIDATE The role of President Josiah Bartlet on NBC's *The West Wing* was tailor-made for Martin Sheen. Both are feisty advocates of liberal causes, though Sheen, a self-described "Catholic radical," seems to pull fewer punches. He has criticized President George W. Bush as "a spoiled-rotten kid who . . . doesn't have a heart." As a father, Sheen has shown tough love to his actor sons Emilio Estevez and Charlie Sheen—once turning in Charlie, now drug-free, for violating his probation. Sheen the elder has himself been busted more than 70 times for antinuclear and other protests. In 1989, when appointed honorary mayor of Malibu (where he still resides with his artist wife, Janet), Sheen declared the city "a nuclear-free zone [and] a sanctuary for aliens and the homeless." Born Ramon Estevez in Dayton, Ohio, one of 10 children of immigrant parents (his dad was Spanish, his mom Irish), Sheen got his start playing outlaws: a subway mugger in *The Incident* (his 1967 film debut), a spree killer in *Badlands,* a military assassin in *Apocalypse Now.* He prepared for his present Oval Office gig by portraying JFK in the 1983 miniseries *Kennedy* and a White House adviser in 1995's *The American President.* The latter's screenwriter, *West Wing* creator Aaron Sorkin, was impressed enough to draft Sheen as Bartlet in 1999. "He has taken on this role so completely," said costar Allison Janney, "that he *is* President as far as I'm concerned."

DYLAN McDERMOTT

Born: October 26, 1961

LEGAL EAGLE "Certain actors, they just show up and—boom!—they've arrived," said Dylan McDermott. "I was never that guy." Indeed, though he scored as Julia Roberts's spouse in *Steel Magnolias* (and, briefly, as her offscreen fiancé) and Clint Eastwood's Secret Service partner in *In the Line of Fire,* it wasn't until his small-screen series debut in 1997 that McDermott enjoyed his sonic boom. As Boston defense attorney Bobby Donnell on ABC's *The Practice,* he became a female-viewer magnet. "Women under 40 want to marry him," said coexecutive producer Jeffrey Kramer, "and women over 40 want to adopt him." (In fact, McDermott's stepmother, Eve Ensler, author of the one-woman show *The Vagina Monologues,* adopted him when he was 19.)

During its first six seasons, the ensemble courtroom drama, with the mercurial, driven Bobby at its hub, built a cult following. His success was no surprise to McDermott. "Instinctively I thought I'd do well in television because I had grown up in front of it," said the Connecticut-born star. "I was a lonely latchkey kid who watched day and night." He was 5 when his mother, then separated from his father, died from an accidental-gunshot wound. After moving to Manhattan to live with his dad, a saloon owner, McDermott enrolled as a drama major at Fordham University and launched himself in a 1977 Off-Broadway play written by his stepmom. A decade later he made the leap to film as a Vietnam grunt in *Hamburger Hill.* In 2001 he was back on the big screen in *Texas Rangers.* "He looks really rugged and masculine," said his wife, actress Shiva Afshar, with whom he has a daughter, Colette. "But inside he's a soft poet."

TEEN DREAMS

THE KIDS WERE ALL RIGHT—FROM BEVERLY HILLS' DASHING DYLAN TO BROOKLYN'S VINNIE BARBARINO AND THAT OTHERWORLDLY, BUTT-KICKING BUFFY . . . YOUTH WAS NOT WASTED ON THESE YOUNG FULFILLERS OF FANTASY

ASHTON KUTCHER

Born: February 7, 1978

GORGEOUS GOOFBALL Hate him because he's beautiful? No way. Ashton Kutcher brought such innate amiability to *That '70s Show* that he managed to make even plaid pants and feathered hair cute again as a dim—if warmhearted and hunky—Wisconsin teen. Keeping his own locks shaggy enough to sport the David Cassidy look "has been bumming me out," admitted the former Calvin Klein model. But the do was the only cloud in an otherwise sunny five-season run (and counting) on FOX. "He got the role because everyone else was reading the character as stupid, but Ashton made him naive," explained series co-creator Bonnie Turner. Plus, "he knocked us out with the way he looked." Young girls agreed, making the chatty Cedar Rapids native—a onetime biochem major at the U of Iowa—into a teen magazine staple and movie natural. *Dude, Where's My Car?* perfectly highlighted his good-natured goofiness; *Just Married* revealed a flair for physical comedy (and spawned a high-profile six-month romance with costar Brittany Murphy). "I know I'll never be the best actor because there's always going to be someone who's been doing it longer," he said. "But no way anybody can work harder than me." Having endured skinning deer in the frigid winter and a summer job sweeping the floors of a Cheerios plant, Kutcher knew a cool calling when he found it. "How are you going to beat a job where you go and hang out with your friends all week and then on Friday somehow you make a TV show? And make people laugh for a living?" he asked. "That's a great job, man."

JOHN STAMOS

Born: August 19, 1963

SWOON MAKER As sweetly sexy Uncle Jesse on ABC's *Full House,* John Stamos played it more silly than sizzling. "Before every kissing scene, he'd eat Doritos and puff on a cigar," said costar Lori Loughlin. The Cypress, California, native started honing his heartthrob mojo in 1982 as Blackie on ABC's *General Hospital.* Two years later the avid drummer landed the series *Dreams,* about an aspiring rocker. It ended quickly, but he was soon living his own dream, touring with the Beach Boys. Finally, after a brief stint on *You Again?,* with TV vet Jack Klugman, came *Full House* in 1987. By the end of its eight-year run, Stamos got antsy. "I wasn't growing," he said, "and I became somewhat of a recluse." He broke out in his 1995 Broadway debut, *How to Succeed in Business Without Really Trying.* Said producer John Hart: "He has a flair for physical comedy that evokes Dean Martin and Cary Grant." In 2001, after the short-lived series *Thieves,* he returned to the stage in *Cabaret,* to glowing reviews. Once involved with Paula Abdul, he now lives on a ranch outside L.A. with his wife, model/actress Rebecca Romijn-Stamos. "When I was a kid," he said, "I wanted to be famous, to be on a sitcom and to have an amazing wife." Sounds like a dream come true.

HAIR TODAY . . . It was the chop heard around the world. Snipping off her trademark locks for *Felicity*'s second season, Keri Russell didn't anticipate the drastic effect on her fans. Viewership quickly fell on the WB series, which had enjoyed solid Nielsens and continuing buzz. (It was so hyped pre-premiere that someone suggested it be retitled ***Publicity.***) "Nobody is cutting their hair again on our network," decreed WB entertainment president Susanne Daniels. Ratings eventually rebounded, and the series lasted four years before ending in 2002. Russell had started as a Mouseketeer when she was 15, alongside Britney Spears, Justin Timberlake and Christina Aguilera. Three years later, she moved to Los Angeles and got bit parts in films before auditioning for *Felicity.* "The character was always intended to be played by someone who was plain looking," said executive producer J.J. Abrams. "Keri was too attractive to play Felicity, yet she couldn't have been more right." (Russell wound up winning a Golden Globe for the role.) During the final season, she also appeared in ***We Were Soldiers*** with Mel Gibson, and has since been reportedly considered as Lois Lane in a future ***Superman*** remake. Not that Russell is fretting the future. "My best friends in life are people who admit they don't have everything figured out, no matter what age they are," she has said. "I hope I never stop doing that either."

KERI RUSSELL

Born: March 23, 1976

SARAH MICHELLE GELLAR

Born: April 14, 1977

VAMPY VANQUISHER She slayed 'em, all right. Trying bravely to survive both high school and attacks by the Undead—equally problematic in the ironically hip, teen-centric worldview of *Buffy the Vampire Slayer*—Sarah Michelle Gellar was a new kind of heroine: a campy beauty who kicked serious butt. "This is a show that stresses individuality, and I think girls can really relate to it," said Gellar, but for seven seasons boys were similarly susceptible to the cult hit's innovative mix of wit, danger, action and a comely cast sporting way cool clothes. "Sarah's got that TV-star thing. You feel a kinship," explained series creator Joss Whedon, even as Buffy endured such unlikely teen trauma as losing her virginity to a 242-year-old vampire named Angel and having to high-kick demons back into hell on her way to homeroom. The New York City native, raised by a single mother and dubbed "the little pro" by castmates, was exactly that, having acted in commercials since the age of 4, after she was spotted by an agent in a restaurant. At 18 she won a daytime Emmy as Susan Lucci's conniving daughter on *All My Children*. "I'm more focused and confident than Buffy," declared Gellar, who put her long years of tae kwon do to good use performing much of her own stunt work in the constant fight scenes. Between shooting seasons, she got a succession of roles in movies like *Scream 2* and *I Know What You Did Last Summer.* On the set of the latter in 1997 she met actor Freddie Prinze Jr., and the two appeared together in the film version of *Scooby-Doo* before their 2002 marriage in Mexico. "Sarah's a sexy firecracker, super witty and really on top of things," said *Last Summer* costar Jennifer Love Hewitt. And on the rare occasions when she is not? "Sometimes when I feel sorry for myself I think, What kind of quip would Buffy come up with here?" Gellar admitted. "That helps."

VALERIE BERTINELLI

Born: April 23, 1960

BROWN-EYED GIRL When Norman Lear picked her from a cattle-call audition to play Barbara Cooper on *One Day at a Time,* Valerie Bertinelli was a 14-year-old L.A. schoolgirl with only a few commercials to her credit. "I got a career handed to me whether I liked it or not," she said. "It completely changed my life." As the headstrong younger daughter of a divorcée (Bonnie Franklin), the effervescent apple-cheeked brunette quickly ascended the ranks of America's Most Adored, and by 20 had wed rock star Eddie Van Halen. When the sitcom ended in 1984, she turned to TV movies and formed her own production company. But it was her turbulent 20-year good-girl/bad-boy marriage—and separation in 2001—that kept her public enthralled. After a hiatus to raise their son Wolfgang, Bertinelli went back to work for two seasons as neophyte seraph Gloria in CBS's *Touched by an Angel,* a part written for her. The show's heavenly motifs, she explained, were "a nice reminder every day that God is around us. Sometimes I need that reminder when life gets a little too crazy."

Born: March 8, 1977

JAMES VAN DER BEEK

SQUARE SWEETIE "I can't have any facial hair," said James Van Der Beek. "Sometimes I have to shave three times a day." And you thought being an adolescent Adonis was easy. Van Der Beek's cheeky, soulful charisma is a main reason that *Dawson's Creek* was a teen must-see from 1998 to '03. Critics complained that the WB's prime-time *Peyton Place* for the Clearasil set had a preoccupation with sex. (One overheated high schooler told a teacher, "You blew it, lady, 'cause I'm the best sex you'll never have.") Van Der Beek, who starred as straight-shooting Dawson Leery, understood his millions of fans: "No one under 20 has said, 'That's too much sex; that's not the way it really is.' " But like his character, the Connecticut native is no hedonist. He made National Honor Society in prep school while, at 17, appearing in an Edward Albee play Off-Broadway. He's "sweet and earnest," said Joshua Jackson (who costarred as Pacey Witter). "He's the good-looking, polite kid who says 'sir' and 'ma'am.' " Van Der Beek, who is engaged to actress Heather McComb, has capitalized on his *Creek* chic with star turns in *Varsity Blues* and *The Rules of Attraction.* Still, he keeps a wary eye on his future. "The problem with teen idols is they grow up," he observed. "I'm trying to establish myself as an actor as opposed to a novelty. I don't know if it'll work."

KATIE HOLMES

Born: December 18, 1978

THE INGENUE Katie Holmes had graduated (with honors) from her strict, all-girls Catholic high school in Toledo only weeks before she landed in *Dawson's Creek* without the proverbial paddle. "A lot of days I just feel like, What am I doing here?" she admitted. What she was doing was playing gorgeous tomboy Joey Potter—the girl next door to Dawson himself—with tortured sarcasm and lovelorn angst. With its frank sex talk, broken families and topical issues, "the show was like lightning in a bottle, and we caught it just when the whole teen thing exploded," said Holmes, who lived much of the year in Wilmington, North Carolina, where the WB series was shot. (The self-described "control freak" had her own condo near the set for most of the six-season run.) Building on her one pre-*Creek* film credit, *The Ice Storm,* Holmes sidestepped the callow youth rut and held out for serious roles, notably as Michael Douglas's college temptress in *Wonder Boys*. "*Dawson's Creek* put me in a box, and that got me out," she said. Concurred *Dawson's* creator, Kevin Williamson: "Katie is not going to get lost as a kid actor. She is so statuesque, graceful and funny. She's also becoming extremely sexy. She is not my little Katie anymore." But not to worry. *Creek* costar Joshua Jackson, who dated Holmes during the show's first season, noted, "Katie is very clean-cut. The wild Katie is still something any parent can be proud of." Her attorney father, homemaker mom and brother could not bring themselves to see her first topless love scene, in the suspense thriller *The Gift.* That threshold to maturity crossed, the baby of the family (which includes three older sisters) has been quietly dating actor Chris Klein (*American Pie*) for three years. This year she once again deferred her college acceptance (to Columbia) and tackled a film remake of the British cult fave *The Singing Detective*. "Katie's being incredibly smart this early in her career," said its director, Keith Gordon. "People will start thinking of her as that great actress rather than that beautiful girl."

Born: October 11, 1966

LUKE PERRY

THE PENSIVE PINUP He had no idea what he was getting into. After just one year of playing *Beverly Hills, 90210*'s resident brooder Dylan McKay, Luke Perry was receiving 3,000 fan letters a week. Public appearances soon became impossible—he once had to escape a mob of 4,000 screaming girls by hiding in a laundry hamper—and at a mall event in 1991, 21 people were injured when a crowd of 10,000 caught a glimpse of the sideburned star. "It must have seemed like a phenomenon," Perry said of the FOX high school drama, which dealt with such heavy topics as divorce, drug abuse and date rape. "But for us, it was just a job." It was a job that soon grew tiresome for Perry, even though he was laying asphalt a week before joining Jason Priestley and Shannen Doherty on the L.A. set. When he left the show after six seasons, casting directors weren't nearly as smitten with the Fredericktown, Ohio, native as his fans, and three years later he made a return to the nation's favorite zip code. "I went back for emotional and financial reasons," he said. "I missed working with those people, and then the producers made it worth my while." Perry recently separated from his wife of 10 years, Minnie Sharp, with whom he has two children. After *90210*'s finale in 2000, he did a well-received stint on the HBO prison drama *Oz,* and he is currently the star of the Showtime sci-fi series *Jeremiah*. "People," Perry has said, "have only seen a very small part of the work that hopefully I'm capable of doing."

CHRISTINA APPLEGATE

Born: November 25, 1971

NAUGHTY NYMPHET As tube-topped, miniskirted high school floozy Kelly Bundy on *Married . . . with Children,* Christina Applegate belied her smarts by playing a nitwit who routinely bungled the English language ("I hope he doesn't make a testicle of himself"). But with the rest of the dysfunctional Bundy family, she helped score a runaway hit for FOX in 1987 and raise TV's raunchiness level in the Cosby-family era. "*Married* broke the rule of sugar-coated television during its time," observed Applegate. "After us came shows like *Roseanne.* We definitely opened the door for profanity and vulgarity on television." Though it never won an Emmy and stirred outrage from the religious right, "the ugly stepchild of Hollywood" (as the cast called *Married*) hung in for 10 years. "It gave people an opportunity to look at how not to be," quipped its precocious star. Applegate was only 15 when she landed the breakout role but already a vet. Her career began at 3 months when she appeared in the arms of her mother, actress Nancy Priddy, on NBC's *Days of Our Lives.* By age 7 she had earned enough money to buy a house, and at 16 dropped out of high school to focus on the job. "I am the typical L.A. story," she has said, "an only child in a single-parent house. [Priddy divorced Christina's record-producer dad, Robert Applegate.] I always had to work, so I've been acting since I could talk. I feel it's really the only thing I'm meant to do in this life, except eventually become a mother and raise a family." Two years ago, she married actor Johnathon Schaech (*That Thing You Do!*), whom she called "the most grounded, glorious human being." After her short-lived sitcom *Jesse* was canceled in 2000, Applegate moved smoothly into feature films including *The Sweetest Thing* with Cameron Diaz. "We've seen Christina for years on TV, so everybody knows she's got amazing comedic timing," said Diaz. "But what's wonderful is she still has the capacity to surprise you. She can do anything if she gets the chance."

JOHN TRAVOLTA

Born: February 18, 1954

STAYIN' ALIVE "Up your nose with a rubber hose." Judging from his favorite line, Vinnie Barbarino, played to the rafters by 21-year-old John Travolta, didn't have much of a way with words, but he was by far the toughest and coolest of the streetwise Sweathogs on *Welcome Back, Kotter.* The antics of the Brooklyn high school remedial class charmed viewers in the late '70s, and provided a national showcase for the singer/dancer/actor from New Jersey. Travolta's Vinnie started out as a swaggering bully on the ABC sitcom but evolved into a sweeter and sexier teen idol who even rose to No. 10 on the *Billboard* charts with a Vinniesque single titled *Let Her In.* For the real-life high school dropout, *Kotter* kicked off a career that was to have more ups and downs than his fleet of three jets. Fearing that he would be typecast and stuck in TV land, he didn't mention that credit when he auditioned for the '76 big-screen cult classic *Carrie.* "I didn't tell anyone I was on a series," he said, "thinking there would be prejudice." In any case, he nailed a featured role. He got his first Oscar nod for his indelible polyester pose in 1977's *Saturday Night Fever,* and was the one that we wanted the following year in *Grease.* After those hits, recalled onetime flame Marilu Henner, "it could be a role for an 80-year-old woman, and John would be offered it." Not for long. After 1980's *Urban Cowboy,* the actor languished for nearly a decade in forgotten films. "It's hard to make a cultural phenomenon every time," Travolta mused of his epochal earlier parts, and he attributed his perseverance through the subsequent drought to his belief in Scientology.

His percentage of the royalties from his soundtrack albums enabled him to continue as, in the words of an insider, "a millionaire who lives like a billionaire." He returned to pop radar screens with 1989's romantic comedy *Look Who's Talking*, and earned his second Oscar nod for his riveting portrayal of a heroin-hopped hit man in *Pulp Fiction.* Older, a little broader in the beam and more watchable than ever, he kept the hits coming: *Phenomenon, The General's Daughter, Get Shorty*. Travolta, who pilots his planes between four homes he shares with his actress wife of 12 years, Kelly Preston, and their two children, rarely thinks about his icon status. Said he: "I wouldn't know what it's like at this point not to be one."

INDEX

PHOTO CREDITS

FRONT COVER (Aniston) Warner Bros./Zuma Press; (Clooney) Matthew Peyton/Getty Images; (Winfrey) ©2002 Fabrizio Ferri/Harpo Productions Inc., all rights reserved. Softcover only: (Romano) Fergus Greer/Icon Int'l.; (Messing) Hahn-Petit-Nebinger/Abaca Press; (Seinfeld) Visages

BACK COVER (Parker) Sante D'Orazio/HBO/Globe Photos; (Moore) Bob Willoughby/MPTV; (Seinfeld) Visages; (White) Mario Casilli/MPTV; (Messing) Hahn-Petit-Nebinger/Abaca Press

TABLE OF CONTENTS **2-3** Lawrence Schwartzwald/Splash News

INTRODUCTION **4-5** Trinette Reed/Corbis

ICONS **6-7** Supplied by Globe Photos **8-9** Janette Beckman/Retna Ltd.; Ken Whitmore/MPTV **10-11** Douglas Kirkland/Corbis Outline **12-13** FOX; NBC **14-15** CBS/Landov; Shonna Valeska **16-17** ©2002 Fabrizio Ferri/Harpo Productions Inc., all rights reserved; Rob Levine/Shooting Star **18-19** Ted Thai/Timepix **20-21** Richard Fish/ Shooting Star; Bob Willoughby/MPTV **22-23** Maddy Miller

MAKING THEIR MARK
24-25 Paramount/Kobal Collection **26-27** Bill Eppridge/Timepix; Bernard Boudreau/Shooting Star **28-29** Andrew Eccles/JBG; ABC Photo Archive **30-31** Jim McHugh/Corbis Outline; Greg Gorman/FOX/Kobal Collection **32-33** (clockwise from left) John Engstead/MPTV; Landov/CBS; Dewey Nicks/Corbis Outline

SITCOM SENSATIONS **34-35** Gail Albert Halaban/Corbis Saba **36-37** Gale M. Adler/Paramount **38-39** Frank Veronsky; Rob Brown/Corbis Outline **40-41** Photofest (2) **42-43** Tony Costa/Corbis Outline **44-45** CBS Photo Archive; ABC Photo Archive **46-47** NBC/Globe Photos (2)

THEY STARTED IN STAND-UP
48-49 Corbis Bettman **50-51** Mark Sennet/Shooting Star; Ian White/Corbis Outline **52-53** (clockwise from left) Dick Zimmerman/Shooting Star; Owen Franken/Corbis Outline; Davis Factor/Corbis Outline **54-55** Bill Bernstein/Corbis Outline; Douglas Kirkland/Corbis Sygma **56-57** (clockwise from top left) Photofest; Bob Sebree; Michael Grecco/Icon Int'l.

BEFORE THEY WERE MOVIE STARS **58-59** (from left) ABC Photo Archive; Neal Peters Collection; NBC/Globe Photos **60-61** (clockwise from top left) Photofest; Everett Collection; Screenscenes; Andrew Semel/FOX **62-63** (clockwise from top left) Screenscenes; ABC Photo Archive (2) **64-65** (from left) Everett Collection; ABC Photo Archive; Photofest **66-67** (clockwise from top left) NBC/Globe Photos; MPTV; ABC Photo Archive (2) **68-69** (clockwise from top left) Ron Tom/FOX; Everett Collection; NBC/Globe Photos; Photofest **70-71** (clockwise from left) Everett Collection (2); ABC Photo Archive; CBS/Landov

STARRING AS THEMSELVES
72-73 Andrew Eccles/JBG **74-75** (from left) Greg Watermann/Corbis Outline; Photofest; Douglas Kirkland/Corbis Outline **76-77** Gregory Heisler/Corbis Outline; Globe Photos **78-79** (clockwise from top left) Tyler Demogenes/Retna Ltd.; Karen Hoyt/Imagedirect/Getty Images; Globe Photos **80-81** Michel Arnaud; Rafael Fuchs

SEXY, SEXY, SEXY **82-83** Stephen Wayda/Corbis Outline **84-85** Bob Frame/Lamoine **86-87** Sante D'Orazio/HBO/Globe Photos **88-89** Bob Noble/Getty Images; NBC/Globe Photos **90-91** Steve Schapiro **92-93** Charles William Bush/Shooting Star; Michael Grecco/Icon Int'l. **94-95** Ken Regan/Camera 5 **96-97** Mark Liddell/Icon Int'l.; Steve Schapiro **98-99** Mario Casilli/MPTV; Maddy Miller

TOUGH CUSTOMERS **100-101** Isabel Snyder/Corbis Outline **102-103** (from left) Screenscenes; Globe Photos; ABC Photo Archive **104-105** (from left) Mark Sennet/Shooting Star; Deborah Feingold/Corbis Outline; Mario Casilli/MPTV **106-107** (clockwise from top left) Globe Photos; Stephen Sigoloff/JBG

SIGNIFICANT OTHERS **108-109** (from left) NBC/Globe Photos; ABC Photo Archive; NBC/Globe Photos **110-111** (clockwise from top left) Screenscenes; Mario Casilli/MPTV; ABC Photo Archive; Globe Photos **112-113** (clockwise from top left) ABC Photo Archive; Screenscenes; Foto Fantasies **114-115** (clockwise from left) Photofest; ABC Photo Archive (2); CBS Photo Archive **116-117** (from left) Photofest (2); Screenscenes

CROWD PLEASERS **118-119** Bill Reitzel/Corbis Outline **120-121** Frank Ockenfels 3/Corbis Outline; Michael Daks/Corbis Outline **122-123** Dana Fineman-Appel/Corbis Sygma; Globe Photos **124-125** Nancy Ellison/Corbis Sygma **126-127** Aaron Rapoport/ Corbis Outline; CBS Photo Archive **128-129** Steve Schapiro; ABC Photo Archive

TEEN DREAMS **130-131** Tony Duran/Corbis Outline **132-133** Steve Schapiro; Robert Fleischauer/Lamoine **134-135** Photofest **136-137** (clockwise from left) MPTV; Photofest; Tony Duran/Corbis Outline **138-139** Mark Sennet/Shooting Star; George Lange/Corbis Outline **140-141** Fridley/RCA Records

CAROLBURNETTCAROLBURN
FOXMICHAELJFOXMICHAELJ
NSOLSENTWINSOLSENTWIN
ARRYHAGMANLARRYHAGMA
DIANESAWYERDIANESAWY
UCEWILLISBRUCEWILLISBRU
DRESCHERFRANDRESCHER
DANZATONYDANZATONYDA
LENDEGENERESELLENDEGEN
TTERJOHNRITTERJOHNRITT
KERIRUSSELLKERIRUSSELL
PERRYLUKEPERRYLUKEPER
EIMARISATOMEIMARISATO
PPJOHNNYDEPPJOHNNYDE
BILLSHEPHERDCYBILLSHEP
EDDIEMURPHYEDDIEMURPH
LONGSHELLEYLONGSHELLEY
YLENOJAYLENOJAYLENOJAY
NAAPPLEGATECHRISTINAAP